It's Time for a GOOD LIFE

I'm Evelyn Tolliver, the founder of Good Life Credit Pros. I launched a credit repair company to empower everyone with the skills & mindset of financial freedom. I'm from an era where things like credit, saving, budgeting and real-life money issues weren't taught. Early in my money making days, I was spending recklessly and never knew the power of my credit. After buying a few houses, cars, and going on lavish vacations and losing it all, I had to start all over again.

I went through this right when the real estate market crashed in 2009-2010, which destroyed my credit, income, and self-confidence. My solution to this problem was learning how to fix credit, build credit, and how to leverage money and credit.. All while getting my self-confidence back with the right mindset. Since I had no real foundation on the power of money or influence of credit, I ended up filing for bankruptcy short sold a home, had a car repossessed, and so much more.

What a tough lesson that was! Teaching myself how to fix all my mistakes by learning the hard way. Once I learned from my mistake, I helped family and friends start repairing and rebuilding their credit. I saw the need to educate them on exactly how the power of credit works and how if you leveraging it will have lifelong benefits! Then boom my business was born Good Life Credit Pros.

I want everyday people to be empowered to live the Good Life. It is my mission to enrich the lives of everyday people within my community and beyond by teaching the power of credit, financial principles, money management, the important life skills and mindset I did not learn in school! I want all of you reaching for your goals of home ownership, owning a business, and leaving a legacy for future generations.

Be blessed and prosperous!

Evelyn

MY Good Life Made Easy

BUDGET & LIFE PLANNER

CREATED BY: EVELYN TOLLIVER

Belongs To

____

____

Oath of Manifestation

As of TODAY, I accept and receive unexpected GOOD, unexpected MONEY, unexpected LOVE, unexpected KINDNESS, unexpected GENEROSITY, unexpected OFFERS, and unexpected PROSPERITY, to begin coming in unexpected ways from unexpected places in my life and the life of others that are around me. I am constantly guided and boldly empowered to receive the lavish abundance that the universe has been holding for me.

I accept the principle that abundance and prosperity have already been given to me. My acceptance of this makes it relay and opens the space for manifestation to RUSH in. I open wide the doors of my consciousness to receive and to give! IT IS DONE NOW!

Through this oath of manifestation, ALL things are possible! I declare that I absolutely live in a friendly universe that is always providing for me. I feel it powerfully happening now! I'm open to receive more abundance and to give more abundance than I have ever experienced before.

I CAN afford ANYTHING I desire! In fact, I am so prosperous that I never need to worry again! I am grateful for all that I am ready to give! I keep myself lifted in high consciousness NO matter what the appearances may seem!

Sign: ______________________________

Date: ______________________________

God is all there is!
So it is!

Manifestations

Saving for a GOOD LIFE

A good life takes some work to get. I learned that saving has been a big piece to get the life I dreamed about. Let's start there with planning for your good life.

What are MY money savings goals?

I will save $ ____________ by ____________ !

What am I saving for?

Why is this important to me?

What ways am I going to save?

How reaching my goal will make me feel?

GOOD LIFE *Savings Tracker*

Shade in the jar as you put away the savings

Amount: **YOU MADE IT!** **Date:**

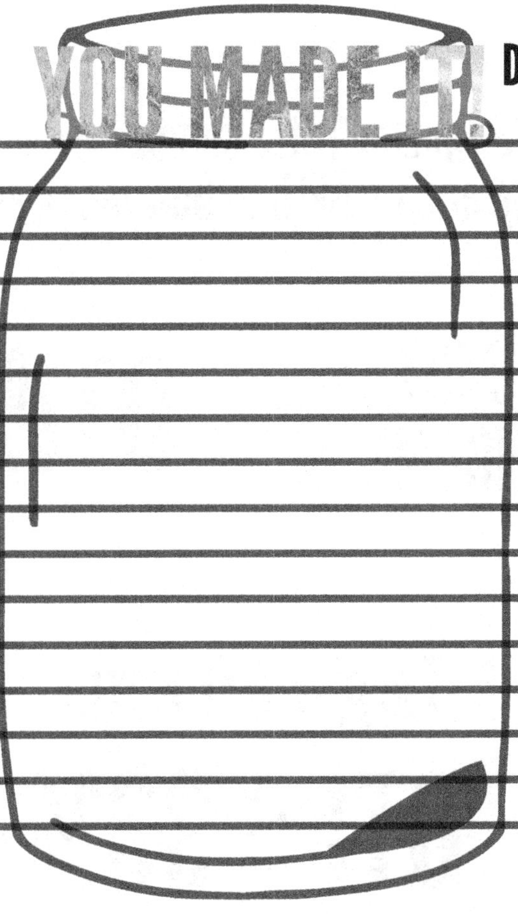

$
$
$
$
$
$
$
$
$
$
$
$
$
$
$
$

GOAL:

Debt Free *Made Easy*

Now it is time to work on getting your debt under control. The key to healthy finances is maintaining a good debt-to-income ratio. To get approved for a mortgage, you will need a debt-to-income ratio showing your financially able to handle taking on more debt. So what is debt-to-income ratio.

Debt-to-Income ratio compares how much you owe each month to how much you earn

$$\frac{\text{DEBT}}{\text{INCOME}} = \text{DTI\%}$$

Target DTI Ratio

$$\text{DTI} \leq 33\%$$

GOOD!

What is your DTI?

Minimum Monthly Credit Card Payment(s) $

Monthly Car Note(s) $

Other Monthly Debt Payment(s) $

Expected Mortgage Payment(s) $

Total Debt:

÷

Monthly Gross Income (Before Taxes & Deductions) $

= Your DTI

Debt TRACKER

DEBT:

GOAL

$

$

Starting Debt on: / /

Debt TRACKER

DEBT:

GOAL

$

$

Starting Debt on: / /

Debt TRACKER

DEBT:

GOAL

$

$

Starting Debt on: / /

Debt TRACKER

DEBT:

GOAL

$

$

Starting Debt on: / /

Emergency Fund *Made Easy*

You need a safety net between you and life!

Don't leave yourself or your family against financial storms... Build up savings.

An emergency fund is important because it serves as insurance for when you face unexpected expenses and/or income shortage. It is smart to always keep at LEAST 6 months worth of budget set aside for an emergency. With the recent COVID-19 pandemic, a years worth of monthly budget may be wiser.

BUDGET Worksheet

INCOME SOURCE	
Paycheck #1	$
Paycheck #2	$
Paycheck #3	$
Paycheck #4	$
Other Income	$
Other Income	$
TOTAL INCOME	$

OFF THE TOP	
Tithe 10%	$
Savings 10%	$
TOTAL	$

PURCHASES	
Groceries	$
Gas	$
Self Care	$
Entertainment	$
Splurge	$
Stash	$
TOTAL	$

EXPENSES	
Rent/Mortgage	$
Utilities	$
Car Note	$
Car Insurance	$
Life Insurance	$
Cable/Satellite	$
Internet	$
Cell Phone	$
Credit Cards	$
Student Loans	$
Miscellaneous	$
TOTAL	$

TOTALS	
"Off The Top" Total	$
"Purchases" Total	$
"Expenses" Total	$
OVERALL TOTAL	$

TOTAL INCOME:

−

OVERALL TOTAL:

EQUALS:

6-Month Fund *Made Easy*

Monthly Budget Total:

$

× 6

Emergency Fund:

$

Pandemic Fund *Made Easy*

Monthly Budget Total:

$

× 12

Emergency Fund:

$

Big Purchase Savings TRACKER

START

When you work hard all year, you SHOULD enjoy a couple of things for yourself. What are 2 big WANTS of yours?

END

Want #1:

Big Purchase Savings TRACKER

START

END

Want #2:

GOOD LIFE

Monthly Plans

NOTES	MONDAY	TUESDAY	WEDNESDAY

MONTH:

THURSDAY	FRIDAY	SATURDAY	SUNDAY

Monthly BUDGET

INCOME	EXPECTED	ACTUAL	DIFFERENCE
HOME EXPENSES			
BUSINESS EXPENSES			

Monthly BUDGET

ADDITIONAL EXPENSES	EXPECTED	ACTUAL	DIFFERENCE

Payment TRACKER

BILL	DUE	$	J	F	M	A	M	J	J	A	S	O	N	D

Self-Development for the month

Books to read this month:

- ○ ______________________________
- ○ ______________________________
- ○ ______________________________

CHAPTERS READ:

MONTHLY HABIT TRACKER

	M	T	W	T	F	S	S
______________________________							
______________________________							
______________________________							
______________________________							
______________________________							

Morning Routine	*Evening Routine*

Monthly Goals CHECK

JAN	FEB	MAR	APR	MAY	JUN	JUL	AUG	SEP	OCT	NOV	DEC

GOAL:

DEADLINE

DATE ACHIEVED

IMPORTANT STEPS:

- ○ ______
- ○ ______
- ○ ______
- ○ ______
- ○ ______
- ○ ______

Manifestations for THIS month:

"Perfection isn't attainable, but if we chase perfection we can catch excellence." - Vince Lombardi

GIRL
BOSS
Hustle

Notes

Girl Code
Boss Up
NOT THAT KIND OF GIRL
EMPOWERED WOMEN
GIRL BOSS

Weekly Goals for

TOP 3

-
-
-

NOTES:

MANIFESTATIONS:

GOOD LIFE Made Easy

"Normal isn't something to aspire to, it's something to get away from." - Jodie Foster

IMPORTANT DATE EVENTS

/
/
/
/
/
/

Weekly TO DO LIST

Monday

Tuesday

Wednesday

Thursday

Friday

Saturday

Sunday

Bonus

GOOD LIFE *Weekly Plans*

MONDAY	TUESDAY	WEDNESDAY	THURSDAY
5AM	5AM	5AM	5AM
6AM	6AM	6AM	6AM
7AM	7AM	7AM	7AM
8AM	8AM	8AM	8AM
9AM	9AM	9AM	9AM
10AM	10AM	10AM	10AM
11AM	11AM	11AM	11AM
12PM	12PM	12PM	12PM
1PM	1PM	1PM	1PM
2PM	2PM	2PM	2PM
3PM	3PM	3PM	3PM
4PM	4PM	4PM	4PM
5PM	5PM	5PM	5PM
6PM	6PM	6PM	6PM
7PM	7PM	7PM	7PM
8PM	8PM	8PM	8PM
9PM	9PM	9PM	9PM
10PM	10PM	10PM	10PM

WEEK:

FRIDAY	SATURDAY	SUNDAY
5AM	5AM	5AM
6AM	6AM	6AM
7AM	7AM	7AM
8AM	8AM	8AM
9AM	9AM	9AM
10AM	10AM	10AM
11AM	11AM	11AM
12PM	12PM	12PM
1PM	1PM	1PM
2PM	2PM	2PM
3PM	3PM	3PM
4PM	4PM	4PM
5PM	5PM	5PM
6PM	6PM	6PM
7PM	7PM	7PM
8PM	8PM	8PM
9PM	9PM	9PM
10PM	10PM	10PM

WEEKLY TO DO

Weekly Goals for

TOP 3

NOTES:

MANIFESTATIONS:

GOOD LIFE *Made Easy*

"Your time is limited, so don't waste it living someone else's life." - Steve Jobs

IMPORTANT DATE EVENTS

/

/

/

/

/

/

Weekly
TO DO LIST

Monday

Tuesday

Wednesday

Thursday

Friday

Saturday

Sunday

Bonus

GOOD LIFE Weekly Plans

MONDAY	TUESDAY	WEDNESDAY	THURSDAY
5AM	5AM	5AM	5AM
6AM	6AM	6AM	6AM
7AM	7AM	7AM	7AM
8AM	8AM	8AM	8AM
9AM	9AM	9AM	9AM
10AM	10AM	10AM	10AM
11AM	11AM	11AM	11AM
12PM	12PM	12PM	12PM
1PM	1PM	1PM	1PM
2PM	2PM	2PM	2PM
3PM	3PM	3PM	3PM
4PM	4PM	4PM	4PM
5PM	5PM	5PM	5PM
6PM	6PM	6PM	6PM
7PM	7PM	7PM	7PM
8PM	8PM	8PM	8PM
9PM	9PM	9PM	9PM
10PM	10PM	10PM	10PM

WEEK:

FRIDAY	SATURDAY	SUNDAY
5AM	5AM	5AM
6AM	6AM	6AM
7AM	7AM	7AM
8AM	8AM	8AM
9AM	9AM	9AM
10AM	10AM	10AM
11AM	11AM	11AM
12PM	12PM	12PM
1PM	1PM	1PM
2PM	2PM	2PM
3PM	3PM	3PM
4PM	4PM	4PM
5PM	5PM	5PM
6PM	6PM	6PM
7PM	7PM	7PM
8PM	8PM	8PM
9PM	9PM	9PM
10PM	10PM	10PM

WEEKLY TO DO

Weekly Goals for

TOP 3

NOTES:

MANIFESTATIONS:

GOOD LIFE Made Easy

"You can't give up! If yo ugive up, you're like everybody else." - Chris Evert

IMPORTANT DATE EVENTS

/

/

/

/

/

/

Weekly TO DO LIST

Monday

Tuesday

Wednesday

Thursday

Friday

Saturday

Sunday

Bonus

GOOD LIFE *Weekly Plans*

MONDAY	TUESDAY	WEDNESDAY	THURSDAY
5AM	5AM	5AM	5AM
6AM	6AM	6AM	6AM
7AM	7AM	7AM	7AM
8AM	8AM	8AM	8AM
9AM	9AM	9AM	9AM
10AM	10AM	10AM	10AM
11AM	11AM	11AM	11AM
12PM	12PM	12PM	12PM
1PM	1PM	1PM	1PM
2PM	2PM	2PM	2PM
3PM	3PM	3PM	3PM
4PM	4PM	4PM	4PM
5PM	5PM	5PM	5PM
6PM	6PM	6PM	6PM
7PM	7PM	7PM	7PM
8PM	8PM	8PM	8PM
9PM	9PM	9PM	9PM
10PM	10PM	10PM	10PM

WEEK:

FRIDAY	SATURDAY	SUNDAY
5AM	5AM	5AM
6AM	6AM	6AM
7AM	7AM	7AM
8AM	8AM	8AM
9AM	9AM	9AM
10AM	10AM	10AM
11AM	11AM	11AM
12PM	12PM	12PM
1PM	1PM	1PM
2PM	2PM	2PM
3PM	3PM	3PM
4PM	4PM	4PM
5PM	5PM	5PM
6PM	6PM	6PM
7PM	7PM	7PM
8PM	8PM	8PM
9PM	9PM	9PM
10PM	10PM	10PM

WEEKLY TO DO

Weekly Goals for

TOP 3

-
-
-

NOTES:

MANIFESTATIONS:

GOOD LIFE Made Easy

"I never dreamed about success. I worked for it." - Este Lauder

IMPORTANT DATE EVENTS

/
/
/
/
/
/

Weekly
TO DO LIST

Monday

Tuesday

Wednesday

Thursday

Friday

Saturday

Sunday

Bonus

GOOD LIFE *Weekly Plans*

MONDAY	TUESDAY	WEDNESDAY	THURSDAY
5AM	5AM	5AM	5AM
6AM	6AM	6AM	6AM
7AM	7AM	7AM	7AM
8AM	8AM	8AM	8AM
9AM	9AM	9AM	9AM
10AM	10AM	10AM	10AM
11AM	11AM	11AM	11AM
12PM	12PM	12PM	12PM
1PM	1PM	1PM	1PM
2PM	2PM	2PM	2PM
3PM	3PM	3PM	3PM
4PM	4PM	4PM	4PM
5PM	5PM	5PM	5PM
6PM	6PM	6PM	6PM
7PM	7PM	7PM	7PM
8PM	8PM	8PM	8PM
9PM	9PM	9PM	9PM
10PM	10PM	10PM	10PM

WEEK:

FRIDAY	SATURDAY	SUNDAY
5AM	5AM	5AM
6AM	6AM	6AM
7AM	7AM	7AM
8AM	8AM	8AM
9AM	9AM	9AM
10AM	10AM	10AM
11AM	11AM	11AM
12PM	12PM	12PM
1PM	1PM	1PM
2PM	2PM	2PM
3PM	3PM	3PM
4PM	4PM	4PM
5PM	5PM	5PM
6PM	6PM	6PM
7PM	7PM	7PM
8PM	8PM	8PM
9PM	9PM	9PM
10PM	10PM	10PM

WEEKLY TO DO

Weekly Goals for

TOP 3

-
-
-

NOTES:

MANIFESTATIONS:

GOOD LIFE Made Easy

"The scariest moment is always right before you start. - Stephen King

IMPORTANT DATE EVENTS

/
/
/
/
/
/

Weekly
TO DO LIST

Monday

Tuesday

Wednesday

Thursday

Friday

Saturday

Sunday

Bonus

GOOD LIFE Weekly Plans

MONDAY	TUESDAY	WEDNESDAY	THURSDAY
5AM	5AM	5AM	5AM
6AM	6AM	6AM	6AM
7AM	7AM	7AM	7AM
8AM	8AM	8AM	8AM
9AM	9AM	9AM	9AM
10AM	10AM	10AM	10AM
11AM	11AM	11AM	11AM
12PM	12PM	12PM	12PM
1PM	1PM	1PM	1PM
2PM	2PM	2PM	2PM
3PM	3PM	3PM	3PM
4PM	4PM	4PM	4PM
5PM	5PM	5PM	5PM
6PM	6PM	6PM	6PM
7PM	7PM	7PM	7PM
8PM	8PM	8PM	8PM
9PM	9PM	9PM	9PM
10PM	10PM	10PM	10PM

WEEK:

FRIDAY	SATURDAY	SUNDAY
5AM	5AM	5AM
6AM	6AM	6AM
7AM	7AM	7AM
8AM	8AM	8AM
9AM	9AM	9AM
10AM	10AM	10AM
11AM	11AM	11AM
12PM	12PM	12PM
1PM	1PM	1PM
2PM	2PM	2PM
3PM	3PM	3PM
4PM	4PM	4PM
5PM	5PM	5PM
6PM	6PM	6PM
7PM	7PM	7PM
8PM	8PM	8PM
9PM	9PM	9PM
10PM	10PM	10PM

WEEKLY TO DO

GOOD LIFE

Monthly Plans

NOTES	MONDAY	TUESDAY	WEDNESDAY

MONTH:

THURSDAY	FRIDAY	SATURDAY	SUNDAY

Monthly BUDGET

INCOME	EXPECTED	ACTUAL	DIFFERENCE
HOME EXPENSES			
BUSINESS EXPENSES			

Monthly BUDGET

ADDITIONAL EXPENSES	EXPECTED	ACTUAL	DIFFERENCE

Payment TRACKER

BILL	DUE	$	J F M A M J J A S O N D

Self-Development for the month

Books to read this month:

- ○ ____________________
- ○ ____________________
- ○ ____________________

CHAPTERS READ:

MONTHLY HABIT TRACKER

M T W T F S S

Morning Routine	Evening Routine

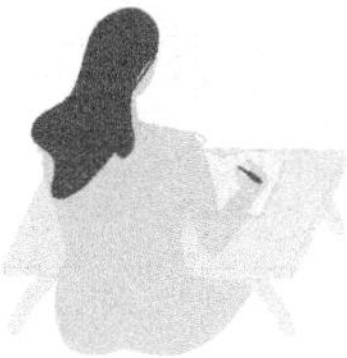

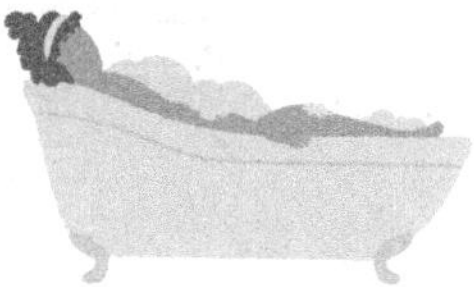

Monthly Goals
CHECK

JAN	FEB	MAR	APR	MAY	JUN	JUL	AUG	SEP	OCT	NOV	DEC

GOAL:

DEADLINE

DATE ACHIEVED

IMPORTANT STEPS:

- [ ] ______
- [ ] ______
- [ ] ______
- [ ] ______
- [ ] ______
- [ ] ______

Manifestations for THIS month:

"Great things are not accomplished by those who yield to trends and facts and popular opinion." - Jack Kerouac

GIRL
BOSS
Hustle

Notes

Girl Code
Boss Up
NOT THAT KIND OF GIRL
EMPOWERED WOMEN
GIRL BOSS

Weekly Goals for

TOP 3

NOTES:

MANIFESTATIONS:

IMPORTANT DATE EVENTS

/

/

/

/

/

/

GOOD LIFE
Made Easy

"The Woman Who Does Not Required Validation From Anyone Is The Most Feared Individual On the Planet." - Mohadesa Najumi

Weekly TO DO LIST

Monday

Tuesday

Wednesday

Thursday

Friday

Saturday

Sunday

Bonus

GOOD LIFE *Weekly Plans*

MONDAY	TUESDAY	WEDNESDAY	THURSDAY
5AM	5AM	5AM	5AM
6AM	6AM	6AM	6AM
7AM	7AM	7AM	7AM
8AM	8AM	8AM	8AM
9AM	9AM	9AM	9AM
10AM	10AM	10AM	10AM
11AM	11AM	11AM	11AM
12PM	12PM	12PM	12PM
1PM	1PM	1PM	1PM
2PM	2PM	2PM	2PM
3PM	3PM	3PM	3PM
4PM	4PM	4PM	4PM
5PM	5PM	5PM	5PM
6PM	6PM	6PM	6PM
7PM	7PM	7PM	7PM
8PM	8PM	8PM	8PM
9PM	9PM	9PM	9PM
10PM	10PM	10PM	10PM

WEEK:

FRIDAY	SATURDAY	SUNDAY
5AM	5AM	5AM
6AM	6AM	6AM
7AM	7AM	7AM
8AM	8AM	8AM
9AM	9AM	9AM
10AM	10AM	10AM
11AM	11AM	11AM
12PM	12PM	12PM
1PM	1PM	1PM
2PM	2PM	2PM
3PM	3PM	3PM
4PM	4PM	4PM
5PM	5PM	5PM
6PM	6PM	6PM
7PM	7PM	7PM
8PM	8PM	8PM
9PM	9PM	9PM
10PM	10PM	10PM

WEEKLY TO DO

Weekly Goals for

TOP 3

-
-
-

NOTES:

MANIFESTATIONS:

GOOD LIFE
Made Easy

Stay Strong.
Make Them Wonder How You're Still Smiling.

IMPORTANT DATE EVENTS

/
/
/
/
/
/

Weekly TO DO LIST

Monday

Tuesday

Wednesday

Thursday

Friday

Saturday

Sunday

Bonus

GOOD LIFE

Weekly Plans

MONDAY	TUESDAY	WEDNESDAY	THURSDAY
5AM	5AM	5AM	5AM
6AM	6AM	6AM	6AM
7AM	7AM	7AM	7AM
8AM	8AM	8AM	8AM
9AM	9AM	9AM	9AM
10AM	10AM	10AM	10AM
11AM	11AM	11AM	11AM
12PM	12PM	12PM	12PM
1PM	1PM	1PM	1PM
2PM	2PM	2PM	2PM
3PM	3PM	3PM	3PM
4PM	4PM	4PM	4PM
5PM	5PM	5PM	5PM
6PM	6PM	6PM	6PM
7PM	7PM	7PM	7PM
8PM	8PM	8PM	8PM
9PM	9PM	9PM	9PM
10PM	10PM	10PM	10PM

WEEK:

FRIDAY	SATURDAY	SUNDAY
5AM	5AM	5AM
6AM	6AM	6AM
7AM	7AM	7AM
8AM	8AM	8AM
9AM	9AM	9AM
10AM	10AM	10AM
11AM	11AM	11AM
12PM	12PM	12PM
1PM	1PM	1PM
2PM	2PM	2PM
3PM	3PM	3PM
4PM	4PM	4PM
5PM	5PM	5PM
6PM	6PM	6PM
7PM	7PM	7PM
8PM	8PM	8PM
9PM	9PM	9PM
10PM	10PM	10PM

WEEKLY TO DO

Weekly Goals for

TOP 3

NOTES:

MANIFESTATIONS:

GOOD LIFE
Made Easy

IMPORTANT DATE EVENTS

/
/
/
/
/
/

I Am Not What Happened To Me.
I Am What I Choose To Become.

Weekly TO DO LIST

Monday

Tuesday

Wednesday

Thursday

Friday

Saturday

Sunday

Bonus

GOOD LIFE *Weekly Plans*

MONDAY	TUESDAY	WEDNESDAY	THURSDAY
5AM	5AM	5AM	5AM
6AM	6AM	6AM	6AM
7AM	7AM	7AM	7AM
8AM	8AM	8AM	8AM
9AM	9AM	9AM	9AM
10AM	10AM	10AM	10AM
11AM	11AM	11AM	11AM
12PM	12PM	12PM	12PM
1PM	1PM	1PM	1PM
2PM	2PM	2PM	2PM
3PM	3PM	3PM	3PM
4PM	4PM	4PM	4PM
5PM	5PM	5PM	5PM
6PM	6PM	6PM	6PM
7PM	7PM	7PM	7PM
8PM	8PM	8PM	8PM
9PM	9PM	9PM	9PM
10PM	10PM	10PM	10PM

WEEK:

FRIDAY	SATURDAY	SUNDAY
5AM	5AM	5AM
6AM	6AM	6AM
7AM	7AM	7AM
8AM	8AM	8AM
9AM	9AM	9AM
10AM	10AM	10AM
11AM	11AM	11AM
12PM	12PM	12PM
1PM	1PM	1PM
2PM	2PM	2PM
3PM	3PM	3PM
4PM	4PM	4PM
5PM	5PM	5PM
6PM	6PM	6PM
7PM	7PM	7PM
8PM	8PM	8PM
9PM	9PM	9PM
10PM	10PM	10PM

WEEKLY TO DO

Weekly Goals for

TOP 3

NOTES:

MANIFESTATIONS:

GOOD LIFE
Made Easy

If I Ever Let My Head Down It Will Be Just To Admire My Shoes.

IMPORTANT DATE EVENTS

/

/

/

/

/

/

Weekly
TO DO LIST

Monday

Tuesday

Wednesday

Thursday

Friday

Saturday

Sunday

Bonus

GOOD LIFE

Weekly Plans

MONDAY	TUESDAY	WEDNESDAY	THURSDAY
5AM	5AM	5AM	5AM
6AM	6AM	6AM	6AM
7AM	7AM	7AM	7AM
8AM	8AM	8AM	8AM
9AM	9AM	9AM	9AM
10AM	10AM	10AM	10AM
11AM	11AM	11AM	11AM
12PM	12PM	12PM	12PM
1PM	1PM	1PM	1PM
2PM	2PM	2PM	2PM
3PM	3PM	3PM	3PM
4PM	4PM	4PM	4PM
5PM	5PM	5PM	5PM
6PM	6PM	6PM	6PM
7PM	7PM	7PM	7PM
8PM	8PM	8PM	8PM
9PM	9PM	9PM	9PM
10PM	10PM	10PM	10PM

WEEK:

FRIDAY	SATURDAY	SUNDAY
5AM	5AM	5AM
6AM	6AM	6AM
7AM	7AM	7AM
8AM	8AM	8AM
9AM	9AM	9AM
10AM	10AM	10AM
11AM	11AM	11AM
12PM	12PM	12PM
1PM	1PM	1PM
2PM	2PM	2PM
3PM	3PM	3PM
4PM	4PM	4PM
5PM	5PM	5PM
6PM	6PM	6PM
7PM	7PM	7PM
8PM	8PM	8PM
9PM	9PM	9PM
10PM	10PM	10PM

NOTES

WEEKLY TO DO

GOOD LIFE

Monthly Plans

NOTES	MONDAY	TUESDAY	WEDNESDAY

MONTH:

THURSDAY	FRIDAY	SATURDAY	SUNDAY

Monthly BUDGET

INCOME	EXPECTED	ACTUAL	DIFFERENCE
HOME EXPENSES			
BUSINESS EXPENSES			

Monthly BUDGET

ADDITIONAL EXPENSES	EXPECTED	ACTUAL	DIFFERENCE

Payment TRACKER

BILL	DUE	$	J	F	M	A	M	J	J	A	S	O	N	D

Self-Development for the month

Books to read this month:

- ______________________________
- ______________________________
- ______________________________

CHAPTERS READ:

MONTHLY HABIT TRACKER

	M	T	W	T	F	S	S

Morning Routine	*Evening Routine*

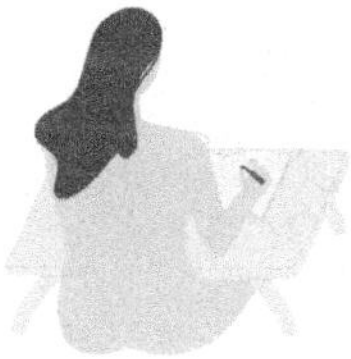

Monthly Goals CHECK

JAN FEB MAR APR MAY JUN JUL AUG SEP OCT NOV DEC

GOAL:

DEADLINE

DATE ACHIEVED

IMPORTANT STEPS:

Manifestations for THIS month:

"A ship is always safe a shore, but that's not what it's built for." - Albert Einstein

GIRL
BOSS
Hustle

Notes

Girl Code
Boss Up
NOT THAT KIND OF GIRL
EMPOWERED WOMEN
GIRL BOSS

Weekly Goals for

TOP 3

-
-
-

NOTES:

MANIFESTATIONS:

GOOD LIFE
Made Easy

This Is The Year I Will Be Stronger. Braver. Kinder. Unstoppable. And This Year I Will Be Fierce.

IMPORTANT DATE EVENTS

/
/
/
/
/
/

Weekly
TO DO LIST

Monday

Tuesday

Wednesday

Thursday

Friday

Saturday

Sunday

Bonus

GOOD LIFE Weekly Plans

MONDAY	TUESDAY	WEDNESDAY	THURSDAY
5AM	5AM	5AM	5AM
6AM	6AM	6AM	6AM
7AM	7AM	7AM	7AM
8AM	8AM	8AM	8AM
9AM	9AM	9AM	9AM
10AM	10AM	10AM	10AM
11AM	11AM	11AM	11AM
12PM	12PM	12PM	12PM
1PM	1PM	1PM	1PM
2PM	2PM	2PM	2PM
3PM	3PM	3PM	3PM
4PM	4PM	4PM	4PM
5PM	5PM	5PM	5PM
6PM	6PM	6PM	6PM
7PM	7PM	7PM	7PM
8PM	8PM	8PM	8PM
9PM	9PM	9PM	9PM
10PM	10PM	10PM	10PM

WEEK:

FRIDAY	SATURDAY	SUNDAY
5AM	5AM	5AM
6AM	6AM	6AM
7AM	7AM	7AM
8AM	8AM	8AM
9AM	9AM	9AM
10AM	10AM	10AM
11AM	11AM	11AM
12PM	12PM	12PM
1PM	1PM	1PM
2PM	2PM	2PM
3PM	3PM	3PM
4PM	4PM	4PM
5PM	5PM	5PM
6PM	6PM	6PM
7PM	7PM	7PM
8PM	8PM	8PM
9PM	9PM	9PM
10PM	10PM	10PM

WEEKLY TO DO

Weekly Goals for

TOP 3

NOTES:

MANIFESTATIONS:

GOOD LIFE Made Easy

Believe In Yourself A Little More.

IMPORTANT DATE EVENTS

/

/

/

/

/

/

Weekly
TO DO LIST

Monday

Tuesday

Wednesday

Thursday

Friday

Saturday

Sunday

Bonus

GOOD LIFE Weekly Plans

MONDAY	TUESDAY	WEDNESDAY	THURSDAY
5AM	5AM	5AM	5AM
6AM	6AM	6AM	6AM
7AM	7AM	7AM	7AM
8AM	8AM	8AM	8AM
9AM	9AM	9AM	9AM
10AM	10AM	10AM	10AM
11AM	11AM	11AM	11AM
12PM	12PM	12PM	12PM
1PM	1PM	1PM	1PM
2PM	2PM	2PM	2PM
3PM	3PM	3PM	3PM
4PM	4PM	4PM	4PM
5PM	5PM	5PM	5PM
6PM	6PM	6PM	6PM
7PM	7PM	7PM	7PM
8PM	8PM	8PM	8PM
9PM	9PM	9PM	9PM
10PM	10PM	10PM	10PM

WEEK:

FRIDAY	SATURDAY	SUNDAY
5AM	5AM	5AM
6AM	6AM	6AM
7AM	7AM	7AM
8AM	8AM	8AM
9AM	9AM	9AM
10AM	10AM	10AM
11AM	11AM	11AM
12PM	12PM	12PM
1PM	1PM	1PM
2PM	2PM	2PM
3PM	3PM	3PM
4PM	4PM	4PM
5PM	5PM	5PM
6PM	6PM	6PM
7PM	7PM	7PM
8PM	8PM	8PM
9PM	9PM	9PM
10PM	10PM	10PM

WEEKLY TO DO

Weekly Goals for

TOP 3

-
-
-

NOTES:

MANIFESTATIONS:

GOOD LIFE Made Easy

"Above All, Be the Heroine Of Your Life. Not The Victim" - Nora Ephron

IMPORTANT DATE EVENTS

/
/
/
/
/
/

Weekly
TO DO LIST

Monday

Tuesday

Wednesday

Thursday

Friday

Saturday

Sunday

Bonus

GOOD LIFE
Weekly Plans

MONDAY	TUESDAY	WEDNESDAY	THURSDAY
5AM	5AM	5AM	5AM
6AM	6AM	6AM	6AM
7AM	7AM	7AM	7AM
8AM	8AM	8AM	8AM
9AM	9AM	9AM	9AM
10AM	10AM	10AM	10AM
11AM	11AM	11AM	11AM
12PM	12PM	12PM	12PM
1PM	1PM	1PM	1PM
2PM	2PM	2PM	2PM
3PM	3PM	3PM	3PM
4PM	4PM	4PM	4PM
5PM	5PM	5PM	5PM
6PM	6PM	6PM	6PM
7PM	7PM	7PM	7PM
8PM	8PM	8PM	8PM
9PM	9PM	9PM	9PM
10PM	10PM	10PM	10PM

WEEK:

FRIDAY	SATURDAY	SUNDAY
5AM	5AM	5AM
6AM	6AM	6AM
7AM	7AM	7AM
8AM	8AM	8AM
9AM	9AM	9AM
10AM	10AM	10AM
11AM	11AM	11AM
12PM	12PM	12PM
1PM	1PM	1PM
2PM	2PM	2PM
3PM	3PM	3PM
4PM	4PM	4PM
5PM	5PM	5PM
6PM	6PM	6PM
7PM	7PM	7PM
8PM	8PM	8PM
9PM	9PM	9PM
10PM	10PM	10PM

WEEKLY TO DO

Weekly Goals for

TOP 3

NOTES:

MANIFESTATIONS:

GOOD LIFE
Made Easy

Make A Fairy Tale And Go Live In It.

IMPORTANT DATE EVENTS

/

/

/

/

/

/

Weekly TO DO LIST

Monday

Tuesday

Wednesday

Thursday

Friday

Saturday

Sunday

Bonus

GOOD LIFE *Weekly Plans*

MONDAY	TUESDAY	WEDNESDAY	THURSDAY
5AM	5AM	5AM	5AM
6AM	6AM	6AM	6AM
7AM	7AM	7AM	7AM
8AM	8AM	8AM	8AM
9AM	9AM	9AM	9AM
10AM	10AM	10AM	10AM
11AM	11AM	11AM	11AM
12PM	12PM	12PM	12PM
1PM	1PM	1PM	1PM
2PM	2PM	2PM	2PM
3PM	3PM	3PM	3PM
4PM	4PM	4PM	4PM
5PM	5PM	5PM	5PM
6PM	6PM	6PM	6PM
7PM	7PM	7PM	7PM
8PM	8PM	8PM	8PM
9PM	9PM	9PM	9PM
10PM	10PM	10PM	10PM

WEEK:

FRIDAY	SATURDAY	SUNDAY
5AM	5AM	5AM
6AM	6AM	6AM
7AM	7AM	7AM
8AM	8AM	8AM
9AM	9AM	9AM
10AM	10AM	10AM
11AM	11AM	11AM
12PM	12PM	12PM
1PM	1PM	1PM
2PM	2PM	2PM
3PM	3PM	3PM
4PM	4PM	4PM
5PM	5PM	5PM
6PM	6PM	6PM
7PM	7PM	7PM
8PM	8PM	8PM
9PM	9PM	9PM
10PM	10PM	10PM

WEEKLY TO DO

Weekly Goals for

TOP 3

-
-
-

NOTES:

MANIFESTATIONS:

GOOD LIFE Made Easy

"Nothing Can Dim The Light That Shines From Within." - Maya Angelou

IMPORTANT DATE EVENTS

/
/
/
/
/
/

Weekly
TO DO LIST

Monday

Tuesday

Wednesday

Thursday

Friday

Saturday

Sunday

Bonus

GOOD LIFE *Weekly Plans*

MONDAY	TUESDAY	WEDNESDAY	THURSDAY
5AM	5AM	5AM	5AM
6AM	6AM	6AM	6AM
7AM	7AM	7AM	7AM
8AM	8AM	8AM	8AM
9AM	9AM	9AM	9AM
10AM	10AM	10AM	10AM
11AM	11AM	11AM	11AM
12PM	12PM	12PM	12PM
1PM	1PM	1PM	1PM
2PM	2PM	2PM	2PM
3PM	3PM	3PM	3PM
4PM	4PM	4PM	4PM
5PM	5PM	5PM	5PM
6PM	6PM	6PM	6PM
7PM	7PM	7PM	7PM
8PM	8PM	8PM	8PM
9PM	9PM	9PM	9PM
10PM	10PM	10PM	10PM

WEEK:

FRIDAY	SATURDAY	SUNDAY
5AM	5AM	5AM
6AM	6AM	6AM
7AM	7AM	7AM
8AM	8AM	8AM
9AM	9AM	9AM
10AM	10AM	10AM
11AM	11AM	11AM
12PM	12PM	12PM
1PM	1PM	1PM
2PM	2PM	2PM
3PM	3PM	3PM
4PM	4PM	4PM
5PM	5PM	5PM
6PM	6PM	6PM
7PM	7PM	7PM
8PM	8PM	8PM
9PM	9PM	9PM
10PM	10PM	10PM

WEEKLY TO DO

GOOD LIFE

Monthly Plans

NOTES	MONDAY	TUESDAY	WEDNESDAY

MONTH:

THURSDAY	FRIDAY	SATURDAY	SUNDAY

Monthly BUDGET

INCOME	EXPECTED	ACTUAL	DIFFERENCE
HOME EXPENSES			
BUSINESS EXPENSES			

Monthly BUDGET

ADDITIONAL EXPENSES	EXPECTED	ACTUAL	DIFFERENCE

Payment TRACKER

BILL	DUE	$	J	F	M	A	M	J	J	A	S	O	N	D

Self-Development for the month

Books to read this month:

- ○ ______________________________
- ○ ______________________________
- ○ ______________________________

CHAPTERS READ:

MONTHLY HABIT TRACKER

M T W T F S S

Morning Routine	Evening Routine

Monthly Goals CHECK

JAN	FEB	MAR	APR	MAY	JUN	JUL	AUG	SEP	OCT	NOV	DEC

GOAL:

DEADLINE

DATE ACHIEVED

IMPORTANT STEPS:

- ___
- ___
- ___
- ___
- ___
- ___

Manifestations for THIS month:

"Don't look at your feet to see if you are doing it right. Just dance." - Anne Lamott

GIRL
BOSS
Hustle

Notes

Girl Code
Boss Up
NOT THAT KIND OF GIRL
EMPOWERED WOMEN
GIRL BOSS

Weekly Goals for

TOP 3

NOTES:

MANIFESTATIONS:

GOOD LIFE Made Easy

The Only Person You Should Try To Be Better Than, Is The Person You Were Yesterday.

IMPORTANT DATE EVENTS

/
/
/
/
/
/

Weekly
TO DO LIST

Monday	Tuesday	Wednesday	Thursday
○	○	○	○
○	○	○	○
○	○	○	○
○	○	○	○
○	○	○	○
○	○	○	○
○	○	○	○
○	○	○	○
○	○	○	○
○	○	○	○

Friday	Saturday	Sunday	Bonus
○	○	○	○
○	○	○	○
○	○	○	○
○	○	○	○
○	○	○	○
○	○	○	○
○	○	○	○
○	○	○	○
○	○	○	○
○	○	○	○

GOOD LIFE Weekly Plans

MONDAY	TUESDAY	WEDNESDAY	THURSDAY
5AM	5AM	5AM	5AM
6AM	6AM	6AM	6AM
7AM	7AM	7AM	7AM
8AM	8AM	8AM	8AM
9AM	9AM	9AM	9AM
10AM	10AM	10AM	10AM
11AM	11AM	11AM	11AM
12PM	12PM	12PM	12PM
1PM	1PM	1PM	1PM
2PM	2PM	2PM	2PM
3PM	3PM	3PM	3PM
4PM	4PM	4PM	4PM
5PM	5PM	5PM	5PM
6PM	6PM	6PM	6PM
7PM	7PM	7PM	7PM
8PM	8PM	8PM	8PM
9PM	9PM	9PM	9PM
10PM	10PM	10PM	10PM

WEEK:

FRIDAY	SATURDAY	SUNDAY
5AM	5AM	5AM
6AM	6AM	6AM
7AM	7AM	7AM
8AM	8AM	8AM
9AM	9AM	9AM
10AM	10AM	10AM
11AM	11AM	11AM
12PM	12PM	12PM
1PM	1PM	1PM
2PM	2PM	2PM
3PM	3PM	3PM
4PM	4PM	4PM
5PM	5PM	5PM
6PM	6PM	6PM
7PM	7PM	7PM
8PM	8PM	8PM
9PM	9PM	9PM
10PM	10PM	10PM

WEEKLY TO DO

Weekly Goals for

TOP 3

-
-
-

NOTES:

MANIFESTATIONS:

GOOD LIFE
Made Easy

Happiness Is Not A Destination It Is A Way Of Life.

IMPORTANT DATE EVENTS

/
/
/
/
/
/

Weekly TO DO LIST

Monday

- ○
- ○
- ○
- ○
- ○
- ○
- ○
- ○
- ○
- ○

Tuesday

- ○
- ○
- ○
- ○
- ○
- ○
- ○
- ○
- ○
- ○

Wednesday

- ○
- ○
- ○
- ○
- ○
- ○
- ○
- ○
- ○
- ○

Thursday

- ○
- ○
- ○
- ○
- ○
- ○
- ○
- ○
- ○
- ○

Friday

- ○
- ○
- ○
- ○
- ○
- ○
- ○
- ○
- ○
- ○

Saturday

- ○
- ○
- ○
- ○
- ○
- ○
- ○
- ○
- ○
- ○

Sunday

- ○
- ○
- ○
- ○
- ○
- ○
- ○
- ○
- ○
- ○

Bonus

- ○
- ○
- ○
- ○
- ○
- ○
- ○
- ○
- ○
- ○

GOOD LIFE Weekly Plans

MONDAY	TUESDAY	WEDNESDAY	THURSDAY
5AM	5AM	5AM	5AM
6AM	6AM	6AM	6AM
7AM	7AM	7AM	7AM
8AM	8AM	8AM	8AM
9AM	9AM	9AM	9AM
10AM	10AM	10AM	10AM
11AM	11AM	11AM	11AM
12PM	12PM	12PM	12PM
1PM	1PM	1PM	1PM
2PM	2PM	2PM	2PM
3PM	3PM	3PM	3PM
4PM	4PM	4PM	4PM
5PM	5PM	5PM	5PM
6PM	6PM	6PM	6PM
7PM	7PM	7PM	7PM
8PM	8PM	8PM	8PM
9PM	9PM	9PM	9PM
10PM	10PM	10PM	10PM

WEEK:

FRIDAY	SATURDAY	SUNDAY
5AM	5AM	5AM
6AM	6AM	6AM
7AM	7AM	7AM
8AM	8AM	8AM
9AM	9AM	9AM
10AM	10AM	10AM
11AM	11AM	11AM
12PM	12PM	12PM
1PM	1PM	1PM
2PM	2PM	2PM
3PM	3PM	3PM
4PM	4PM	4PM
5PM	5PM	5PM
6PM	6PM	6PM
7PM	7PM	7PM
8PM	8PM	8PM
9PM	9PM	9PM
10PM	10PM	10PM

WEEKLY TO DO

Weekly Goals for

TOP 3

NOTES:

MANIFESTATIONS:

GOOD LIFE
Made Easy

Ask Yourself If What You're Doing Today Is Getting You Closer To Where You Want To Be Tomorrow.

IMPORTANT DATE EVENTS

/
/
/
/
/
/

Weekly
TO DO LIST

Monday

Tuesday

Wednesday

Thursday

Friday

Saturday

Sunday

Bonus

GOOD LIFE

Weekly Plans

MONDAY	TUESDAY	WEDNESDAY	THURSDAY
5AM	5AM	5AM	5AM
6AM	6AM	6AM	6AM
7AM	7AM	7AM	7AM
8AM	8AM	8AM	8AM
9AM	9AM	9AM	9AM
10AM	10AM	10AM	10AM
11AM	11AM	11AM	11AM
12PM	12PM	12PM	12PM
1PM	1PM	1PM	1PM
2PM	2PM	2PM	2PM
3PM	3PM	3PM	3PM
4PM	4PM	4PM	4PM
5PM	5PM	5PM	5PM
6PM	6PM	6PM	6PM
7PM	7PM	7PM	7PM
8PM	8PM	8PM	8PM
9PM	9PM	9PM	9PM
10PM	10PM	10PM	10PM

WEEK:

FRIDAY	SATURDAY	SUNDAY
5AM	5AM	5AM
6AM	6AM	6AM
7AM	7AM	7AM
8AM	8AM	8AM
9AM	9AM	9AM
10AM	10AM	10AM
11AM	11AM	11AM
12PM	12PM	12PM
1PM	1PM	1PM
2PM	2PM	2PM
3PM	3PM	3PM
4PM	4PM	4PM
5PM	5PM	5PM
6PM	6PM	6PM
7PM	7PM	7PM
8PM	8PM	8PM
9PM	9PM	9PM
10PM	10PM	10PM

WEEKLY TO DO

Weekly Goals for

TOP 3

-
-
-

NOTES:

MANIFESTATIONS:

GOOD LIFE
Made Easy

Don't Let Anyone Ever Dull Your Sparkle.

IMPORTANT DATE EVENTS

/
/
/
/
/
/

Weekly
TO DO LIST

Monday

Tuesday

Wednesday

Thursday

Friday

Saturday

Sunday

Bonus

GOOD LIFE *Weekly Plans*

	MONDAY	TUESDAY	WEDNESDAY	THURSDAY
5AM				
6AM				
7AM				
8AM				
9AM				
10AM				
11AM				
12PM				
1PM				
2PM				
3PM				
4PM				
5PM				
6PM				
7PM				
8PM				
9PM				
10PM				

WEEK:

FRIDAY	SATURDAY	SUNDAY
5AM	5AM	5AM
6AM	6AM	6AM
7AM	7AM	7AM
8AM	8AM	8AM
9AM	9AM	9AM
10AM	10AM	10AM
11AM	11AM	11AM
12PM	12PM	12PM
1PM	1PM	1PM
2PM	2PM	2PM
3PM	3PM	3PM
4PM	4PM	4PM
5PM	5PM	5PM
6PM	6PM	6PM
7PM	7PM	7PM
8PM	8PM	8PM
9PM	9PM	9PM
10PM	10PM	10PM

WEEKLY TO DO

GOOD LIFE

Monthly Plans

NOTES

MONDAY

TUESDAY

WEDNESDAY

MONTH:

THURSDAY	FRIDAY	SATURDAY	SUNDAY

Monthly BUDGET

INCOME	EXPECTED	ACTUAL	DIFFERENCE
HOME EXPENSES			
BUSINESS EXPENSES			

Monthly BUDGET

ADDITIONAL EXPENSES	EXPECTED	ACTUAL	DIFFERENCE

Payment TRACKER

BILL	DUE	$	J	F	M	A	M	J	J	A	S	O	N	D

Self-Development for the month

Books to read this month:

- ○ ______________________________
- ○ ______________________________
- ○ ______________________________

CHAPTERS READ:

MONTHLY HABIT TRACKER

	M	T	W	T	F	S	S
______________________________							
______________________________							
______________________________							
______________________________							
______________________________							

Morning Routine	*Evening Routine*
____________________	____________________
____________________	____________________
____________________	____________________
____________________	____________________
____________________	____________________

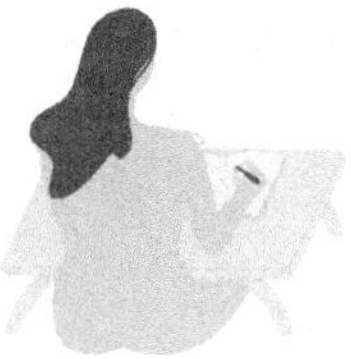

Monthly Goals

CHECK

JAN	FEB	MAR	APR	MAY	JUN	JUL	AUG	SEP	OCT	NOV	DEC

GOAL:

DEADLINE

DATE ACHIEVED

IMPORTANT STEPS:

Manifestations for THIS month:

"In order to be irreplaceable, one must always be different." - CoCo Chanel

GIRL BOSS
Hustle

Notes

Girl Code
Boss Up
NOT THAT KIND OF GIRL
EMPOWERED WOMEN
GIRL BOSS

Weekly Goals for

TOP 3

NOTES:

MANIFESTATIONS:

GOOD LIFE Made Easy

IMPORTANT DATE EVENTS

/
/
/
/
/
/

Having A Soft Heart In A Cruel World Is Courage. Not Weakness.

Weekly TO DO LIST

Monday

Tuesday

Wednesday

Thursday

Friday

Saturday

Sunday

Bonus

GOOD LIFE
Weekly Plans

MONDAY	TUESDAY	WEDNESDAY	THURSDAY
5AM	5AM	5AM	5AM
6AM	6AM	6AM	6AM
7AM	7AM	7AM	7AM
8AM	8AM	8AM	8AM
9AM	9AM	9AM	9AM
10AM	10AM	10AM	10AM
11AM	11AM	11AM	11AM
12PM	12PM	12PM	12PM
1PM	1PM	1PM	1PM
2PM	2PM	2PM	2PM
3PM	3PM	3PM	3PM
4PM	4PM	4PM	4PM
5PM	5PM	5PM	5PM
6PM	6PM	6PM	6PM
7PM	7PM	7PM	7PM
8PM	8PM	8PM	8PM
9PM	9PM	9PM	9PM
10PM	10PM	10PM	10PM

WEEK:

FRIDAY	SATURDAY	SUNDAY
5AM	5AM	5AM
6AM	6AM	6AM
7AM	7AM	7AM
8AM	8AM	8AM
9AM	9AM	9AM
10AM	10AM	10AM
11AM	11AM	11AM
12PM	12PM	12PM
1PM	1PM	1PM
2PM	2PM	2PM
3PM	3PM	3PM
4PM	4PM	4PM
5PM	5PM	5PM
6PM	6PM	6PM
7PM	7PM	7PM
8PM	8PM	8PM
9PM	9PM	9PM
10PM	10PM	10PM

WEEKLY TO DO

Weekly Goals for

TOP 3

-
-
-

NOTES:

MANIFESTATIONS:

IMPORTANT DATE EVENTS

/
/
/
/
/
/

GOOD LIFE
Made Easy

What Ever You Decide To Do, Make Sure It Makes You Happy.

Weekly
TO DO LIST

Monday

Tuesday

Wednesday

Thursday

Friday

Saturday

Sunday

Bonus

GOOD LIFE *Weekly Plans*

MONDAY	TUESDAY	WEDNESDAY	THURSDAY
5AM	5AM	5AM	5AM
6AM	6AM	6AM	6AM
7AM	7AM	7AM	7AM
8AM	8AM	8AM	8AM
9AM	9AM	9AM	9AM
10AM	10AM	10AM	10AM
11AM	11AM	11AM	11AM
12PM	12PM	12PM	12PM
1PM	1PM	1PM	1PM
2PM	2PM	2PM	2PM
3PM	3PM	3PM	3PM
4PM	4PM	4PM	4PM
5PM	5PM	5PM	5PM
6PM	6PM	6PM	6PM
7PM	7PM	7PM	7PM
8PM	8PM	8PM	8PM
9PM	9PM	9PM	9PM
10PM	10PM	10PM	10PM

WEEK:

FRIDAY	SATURDAY	SUNDAY
5AM	5AM	5AM
6AM	6AM	6AM
7AM	7AM	7AM
8AM	8AM	8AM
9AM	9AM	9AM
10AM	10AM	10AM
11AM	11AM	11AM
12PM	12PM	12PM
1PM	1PM	1PM
2PM	2PM	2PM
3PM	3PM	3PM
4PM	4PM	4PM
5PM	5PM	5PM
6PM	6PM	6PM
7PM	7PM	7PM
8PM	8PM	8PM
9PM	9PM	9PM
10PM	10PM	10PM

WEEKLY TO DO

Weekly Goals for

TOP 3

-
-
-

NOTES:

MANIFESTATIONS:

GOOD LIFE Made Easy

"Be a Girl with a mind, a Woman with attitude, and a Lady with class."

IMPORTANT DATE EVENTS

/
/
/
/
/
/

Weekly
TO DO LIST

Monday

Tuesday

Wednesday

Thursday

Friday

Saturday

Sunday

Bonus

GOOD LIFE *Weekly Plans*

MONDAY	TUESDAY	WEDNESDAY	THURSDAY
5AM	5AM	5AM	5AM
6AM	6AM	6AM	6AM
7AM	7AM	7AM	7AM
8AM	8AM	8AM	8AM
9AM	9AM	9AM	9AM
10AM	10AM	10AM	10AM
11AM	11AM	11AM	11AM
12PM	12PM	12PM	12PM
1PM	1PM	1PM	1PM
2PM	2PM	2PM	2PM
3PM	3PM	3PM	3PM
4PM	4PM	4PM	4PM
5PM	5PM	5PM	5PM
6PM	6PM	6PM	6PM
7PM	7PM	7PM	7PM
8PM	8PM	8PM	8PM
9PM	9PM	9PM	9PM
10PM	10PM	10PM	10PM

WEEK:

FRIDAY	SATURDAY	SUNDAY
5AM	5AM	5AM
6AM	6AM	6AM
7AM	7AM	7AM
8AM	8AM	8AM
9AM	9AM	9AM
10AM	10AM	10AM
11AM	11AM	11AM
12PM	12PM	12PM
1PM	1PM	1PM
2PM	2PM	2PM
3PM	3PM	3PM
4PM	4PM	4PM
5PM	5PM	5PM
6PM	6PM	6PM
7PM	7PM	7PM
8PM	8PM	8PM
9PM	9PM	9PM
10PM	10PM	10PM

WEEKLY TO DO

Weekly Goals for

TOP 3

-
-
-

NOTES:

MANIFESTATIONS:

GOOD LIFE Made Easy

Let It All Go. See What Stays.

IMPORTANT DATE EVENTS

/
/
/
/
/
/

Weekly TO DO LIST

Monday

Tuesday

Wednesday

Thursday

Friday

Saturday

Sunday

Bonus

GOOD LIFE

Weekly Plans

MONDAY	TUESDAY	WEDNESDAY	THURSDAY
5AM	5AM	5AM	5AM
6AM	6AM	6AM	6AM
7AM	7AM	7AM	7AM
8AM	8AM	8AM	8AM
9AM	9AM	9AM	9AM
10AM	10AM	10AM	10AM
11AM	11AM	11AM	11AM
12PM	12PM	12PM	12PM
1PM	1PM	1PM	1PM
2PM	2PM	2PM	2PM
3PM	3PM	3PM	3PM
4PM	4PM	4PM	4PM
5PM	5PM	5PM	5PM
6PM	6PM	6PM	6PM
7PM	7PM	7PM	7PM
8PM	8PM	8PM	8PM
9PM	9PM	9PM	9PM
10PM	10PM	10PM	10PM

WEEK:

FRIDAY	SATURDAY	SUNDAY
5AM	5AM	5AM
6AM	6AM	6AM
7AM	7AM	7AM
8AM	8AM	8AM
9AM	9AM	9AM
10AM	10AM	10AM
11AM	11AM	11AM
12PM	12PM	12PM
1PM	1PM	1PM
2PM	2PM	2PM
3PM	3PM	3PM
4PM	4PM	4PM
5PM	5PM	5PM
6PM	6PM	6PM
7PM	7PM	7PM
8PM	8PM	8PM
9PM	9PM	9PM
10PM	10PM	10PM

WEEKLY TO DO

Weekly Goals for

TOP 3

NOTES:

MANIFESTATIONS:

GOOD LIFE *Made Easy*

It Always Seems Impossible Until It's Done.

IMPORTANT DATE EVENTS

/

/

/

/

/

/

Weekly TO DO LIST

Monday

Tuesday

Wednesday

Thursday

Friday

Saturday

Sunday

Bonus

GOOD LIFE Weekly Plans

MONDAY	TUESDAY	WEDNESDAY	THURSDAY
5AM	5AM	5AM	5AM
6AM	6AM	6AM	6AM
7AM	7AM	7AM	7AM
8AM	8AM	8AM	8AM
9AM	9AM	9AM	9AM
10AM	10AM	10AM	10AM
11AM	11AM	11AM	11AM
12PM	12PM	12PM	12PM
1PM	1PM	1PM	1PM
2PM	2PM	2PM	2PM
3PM	3PM	3PM	3PM
4PM	4PM	4PM	4PM
5PM	5PM	5PM	5PM
6PM	6PM	6PM	6PM
7PM	7PM	7PM	7PM
8PM	8PM	8PM	8PM
9PM	9PM	9PM	9PM
10PM	10PM	10PM	10PM

WEEK:

FRIDAY	SATURDAY	SUNDAY
5AM	5AM	5AM
6AM	6AM	6AM
7AM	7AM	7AM
8AM	8AM	8AM
9AM	9AM	9AM
10AM	10AM	10AM
11AM	11AM	11AM
12PM	12PM	12PM
1PM	1PM	1PM
2PM	2PM	2PM
3PM	3PM	3PM
4PM	4PM	4PM
5PM	5PM	5PM
6PM	6PM	6PM
7PM	7PM	7PM
8PM	8PM	8PM
9PM	9PM	9PM
10PM	10PM	10PM

WEEKLY TO DO

GOOD LIFE

Monthly Plans

NOTES	MONDAY	TUESDAY	WEDNESDAY

MONTH:

THURSDAY	FRIDAY	SATURDAY	SUNDAY

Monthly BUDGET

INCOME	EXPECTED	ACTUAL	DIFFERENCE
HOME EXPENSES			
BUSINESS EXPENSES			

Monthly BUDGET

ADDITIONAL EXPENSES	EXPECTED	ACTUAL	DIFFERENCE

Payment TRACKER

BILL	DUE	$	J F M A M J J A S O N D

Self-Development for the month

Books to read this month:

- ○ ______________________________
- ○ ______________________________
- ○ ______________________________

CHAPTERS READ:

MONTHLY HABIT TRACKER

	M	T	W	T	F	S	S
______________							
______________							
______________							
______________							
______________							

Morning Routine	*Evening Routine*
______________	______________
______________	______________
______________	______________
______________	______________
______________	______________

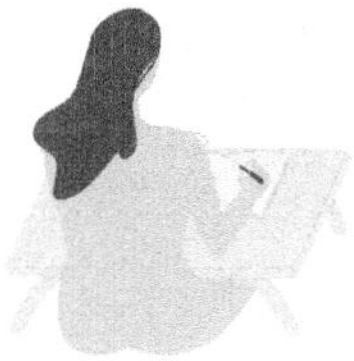

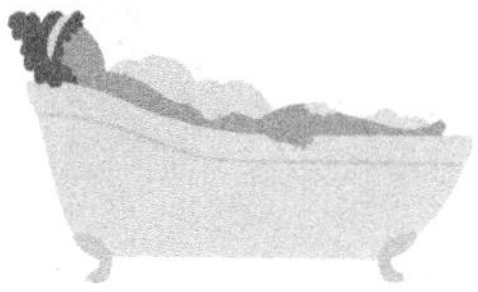

Monthly Goals CHECK

JAN	FEB	MAR	APR	MAY	JUN	JUL	AUG	SEP	OCT	NOV	DEC

GOAL:

DEADLINE **DATE ACHIEVED**

IMPORTANT STEPS:

- ○ __________
- ○ __________
- ○ __________
- ○ __________
- ○ __________
- ○ __________

Manifestations for THIS month:

"When the whole world is silent, even one voice becomes more powerful." - Malala Youdafzai

GIRL
BOSS
Hustle

Notes

Girl Code
Boss Up
NOT THAT KIND OF GIRL
EMPOWERED WOMEN
GIRL BOSS

Weekly Goals for

TOP 3

NOTES:

MANIFESTATIONS:

GOOD LIFE Made Easy

IMPORTANT DATE EVENTS

/

/

/

/

/

/

Don't Call It A Dream Call It A Plan.

Weekly
TO DO LIST

Monday

Tuesday

Wednesday

Thursday

Friday

Saturday

Sunday

Bonus

GOOD LIFE

Weekly Plans

MONDAY	TUESDAY	WEDNESDAY	THURSDAY
5AM	5AM	5AM	5AM
6AM	6AM	6AM	6AM
7AM	7AM	7AM	7AM
8AM	8AM	8AM	8AM
9AM	9AM	9AM	9AM
10AM	10AM	10AM	10AM
11AM	11AM	11AM	11AM
12PM	12PM	12PM	12PM
1PM	1PM	1PM	1PM
2PM	2PM	2PM	2PM
3PM	3PM	3PM	3PM
4PM	4PM	4PM	4PM
5PM	5PM	5PM	5PM
6PM	6PM	6PM	6PM
7PM	7PM	7PM	7PM
8PM	8PM	8PM	8PM
9PM	9PM	9PM	9PM
10PM	10PM	10PM	10PM

WEEK:

FRIDAY	SATURDAY	SUNDAY
5AM	5AM	5AM
6AM	6AM	6AM
7AM	7AM	7AM
8AM	8AM	8AM
9AM	9AM	9AM
10AM	10AM	10AM
11AM	11AM	11AM
12PM	12PM	12PM
1PM	1PM	1PM
2PM	2PM	2PM
3PM	3PM	3PM
4PM	4PM	4PM
5PM	5PM	5PM
6PM	6PM	6PM
7PM	7PM	7PM
8PM	8PM	8PM
9PM	9PM	9PM
10PM	10PM	10PM

WEEKLY TO DO

Weekly Goals for

TOP 3

-
-
-

NOTES:

MANIFESTATIONS:

GOOD LIFE Made Easy

Failure Is The Opportunity To Being Again More Intelligently.

IMPORTANT DATE EVENTS

/
/
/
/
/
/

Weekly TO DO LIST

Monday

Tuesday

Wednesday

Thursday

Friday

Saturday

Sunday

Bonus

GOOD LIFE Weekly Plans

MONDAY	TUESDAY	WEDNESDAY	THURSDAY
5AM	5AM	5AM	5AM
6AM	6AM	6AM	6AM
7AM	7AM	7AM	7AM
8AM	8AM	8AM	8AM
9AM	9AM	9AM	9AM
10AM	10AM	10AM	10AM
11AM	11AM	11AM	11AM
12PM	12PM	12PM	12PM
1PM	1PM	1PM	1PM
2PM	2PM	2PM	2PM
3PM	3PM	3PM	3PM
4PM	4PM	4PM	4PM
5PM	5PM	5PM	5PM
6PM	6PM	6PM	6PM
7PM	7PM	7PM	7PM
8PM	8PM	8PM	8PM
9PM	9PM	9PM	9PM
10PM	10PM	10PM	10PM

WEEK:

FRIDAY	SATURDAY	SUNDAY
5AM	5AM	5AM
6AM	6AM	6AM
7AM	7AM	7AM
8AM	8AM	8AM
9AM	9AM	9AM
10AM	10AM	10AM
11AM	11AM	11AM
12PM	12PM	12PM
1PM	1PM	1PM
2PM	2PM	2PM
3PM	3PM	3PM
4PM	4PM	4PM
5PM	5PM	5PM
6PM	6PM	6PM
7PM	7PM	7PM
8PM	8PM	8PM
9PM	9PM	9PM
10PM	10PM	10PM

WEEKLY TO DO

Weekly Goals for

TOP 3

-
-
-

NOTES:

MANIFESTATIONS:

GOOD LIFE
Made Easy

Everything You Do Now Is For Your Future Think About That.

IMPORTANT DATE EVENTS

/
/
/
/
/
/

Weekly TO DO LIST

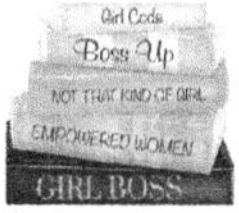

Monday

Tuesday

Wednesday

Thursday

Friday

Saturday

Sunday

Bonus

GOOD LIFE Weekly Plans

MONDAY	TUESDAY	WEDNESDAY	THURSDAY
5AM	5AM	5AM	5AM
6AM	6AM	6AM	6AM
7AM	7AM	7AM	7AM
8AM	8AM	8AM	8AM
9AM	9AM	9AM	9AM
10AM	10AM	10AM	10AM
11AM	11AM	11AM	11AM
12PM	12PM	12PM	12PM
1PM	1PM	1PM	1PM
2PM	2PM	2PM	2PM
3PM	3PM	3PM	3PM
4PM	4PM	4PM	4PM
5PM	5PM	5PM	5PM
6PM	6PM	6PM	6PM
7PM	7PM	7PM	7PM
8PM	8PM	8PM	8PM
9PM	9PM	9PM	9PM
10PM	10PM	10PM	10PM

WEEK:

FRIDAY	SATURDAY	SUNDAY
5AM	5AM	5AM
6AM	6AM	6AM
7AM	7AM	7AM
8AM	8AM	8AM
9AM	9AM	9AM
10AM	10AM	10AM
11AM	11AM	11AM
12PM	12PM	12PM
1PM	1PM	1PM
2PM	2PM	2PM
3PM	3PM	3PM
4PM	4PM	4PM
5PM	5PM	5PM
6PM	6PM	6PM
7PM	7PM	7PM
8PM	8PM	8PM
9PM	9PM	9PM
10PM	10PM	10PM

WEEKLY TO DO

Weekly Goals for

TOP 3

NOTES:

MANIFESTATIONS:

GOOD LIFE Made Easy

"Life Isn't About Finding Yourself. Life Is About Creating Yourself." - George Bernard Shaw

IMPORTANT DATE EVENTS

/

/

/

/

/

/

Weekly TO DO LIST

Monday

Tuesday

Wednesday

Thursday

Friday

Saturday

Sunday

Bonus

GOOD LIFE *Weekly Plans*

MONDAY	TUESDAY	WEDNESDAY	THURSDAY
5AM	5AM	5AM	5AM
6AM	6AM	6AM	6AM
7AM	7AM	7AM	7AM
8AM	8AM	8AM	8AM
9AM	9AM	9AM	9AM
10AM	10AM	10AM	10AM
11AM	11AM	11AM	11AM
12PM	12PM	12PM	12PM
1PM	1PM	1PM	1PM
2PM	2PM	2PM	2PM
3PM	3PM	3PM	3PM
4PM	4PM	4PM	4PM
5PM	5PM	5PM	5PM
6PM	6PM	6PM	6PM
7PM	7PM	7PM	7PM
8PM	8PM	8PM	8PM
9PM	9PM	9PM	9PM
10PM	10PM	10PM	10PM

WEEK:

FRIDAY	SATURDAY	SUNDAY
5AM	5AM	5AM
6AM	6AM	6AM
7AM	7AM	7AM
8AM	8AM	8AM
9AM	9AM	9AM
10AM	10AM	10AM
11AM	11AM	11AM
12PM	12PM	12PM
1PM	1PM	1PM
2PM	2PM	2PM
3PM	3PM	3PM
4PM	4PM	4PM
5PM	5PM	5PM
6PM	6PM	6PM
7PM	7PM	7PM
8PM	8PM	8PM
9PM	9PM	9PM
10PM	10PM	10PM

WEEKLY TO DO

GOOD LIFE

Monthly Plans

NOTES

MONDAY

TUESDAY

WEDNESDAY

MONTH:

THURSDAY	FRIDAY	SATURDAY	SUNDAY

Monthly BUDGET

INCOME	EXPECTED	ACTUAL	DIFFERENCE
HOME EXPENSES			
BUSINESS EXPENSES			

Monthly BUDGET

ADDITIONAL EXPENSES	EXPECTED	ACTUAL	DIFFERENCE

Payment TRACKER

BILL	DUE	$	J F M A M J J A S O N D

Self-Development for the month

Books to read this month:

- ○ ______________________
- ○ ______________________
- ○ ______________________

CHAPTERS READ:

MONTHLY HABIT TRACKER

	M	T	W	T	F	S	S
______________________							
______________________							
______________________							
______________________							
______________________							

Morning Routine	*Evening Routine*
______________________	______________________
______________________	______________________
______________________	______________________
______________________	______________________
______________________	______________________

Monthly Goals
CHECK

JAN	FEB	MAR	APR	MAY	JUN	JUL	AUG	SEP	OCT	NOV	DEC

GOAL:

DEADLINE

DATE ACHIEVED

IMPORTANT STEPS:

Manifestations for THIS month:

"Never limit yourself because of other's limited imaginations: never limit others because of your own unlimited imaginations."" - Mae Jemison

GIRL BOSS
Hustle

Notes

Girl Code
Boss Up
NOT THAT KIND OF GIRL
EMPOWERED WOMEN
GIRL BOSS

Weekly Goals for

TOP 3

NOTES:

MANIFESTATIONS:

IMPORTANT DATE EVENTS

/

/

/

/

/

/

GOOD LIFE
Made Easy

"The question isn't who is going to let me; it's who is going to stop me." – Ayn Rand

Weekly TO DO LIST

Monday

Tuesday

Wednesday

Thursday

Friday

Saturday

Sunday

Bonus

GOOD LIFE
Weekly Plans

MONDAY	TUESDAY	WEDNESDAY	THURSDAY
5AM	5AM	5AM	5AM
6AM	6AM	6AM	6AM
7AM	7AM	7AM	7AM
8AM	8AM	8AM	8AM
9AM	9AM	9AM	9AM
10AM	10AM	10AM	10AM
11AM	11AM	11AM	11AM
12PM	12PM	12PM	12PM
1PM	1PM	1PM	1PM
2PM	2PM	2PM	2PM
3PM	3PM	3PM	3PM
4PM	4PM	4PM	4PM
5PM	5PM	5PM	5PM
6PM	6PM	6PM	6PM
7PM	7PM	7PM	7PM
8PM	8PM	8PM	8PM
9PM	9PM	9PM	9PM
10PM	10PM	10PM	10PM

WEEK:

FRIDAY	SATURDAY	SUNDAY
5AM	5AM	5AM
6AM	6AM	6AM
7AM	7AM	7AM
8AM	8AM	8AM
9AM	9AM	9AM
10AM	10AM	10AM
11AM	11AM	11AM
12PM	12PM	12PM
1PM	1PM	1PM
2PM	2PM	2PM
3PM	3PM	3PM
4PM	4PM	4PM
5PM	5PM	5PM
6PM	6PM	6PM
7PM	7PM	7PM
8PM	8PM	8PM
9PM	9PM	9PM
10PM	10PM	10PM

WEEKLY TO DO

Weekly Goals for

TOP 3

NOTES:

MANIFESTATIONS:

IMPORTANT DATE EVENTS

/

/

/

/

/

/

GOOD LIFE Made Easy

"A girl should be two things: classy and fabulous." - Coco Chanel

Weekly
TO DO LIST

Monday

Tuesday

Wednesday

Thursday

Friday

Saturday

Sunday

Bonus

GOOD LIFE

Weekly Plans

MONDAY	TUESDAY	WEDNESDAY	THURSDAY
5AM	5AM	5AM	5AM
6AM	6AM	6AM	6AM
7AM	7AM	7AM	7AM
8AM	8AM	8AM	8AM
9AM	9AM	9AM	9AM
10AM	10AM	10AM	10AM
11AM	11AM	11AM	11AM
12PM	12PM	12PM	12PM
1PM	1PM	1PM	1PM
2PM	2PM	2PM	2PM
3PM	3PM	3PM	3PM
4PM	4PM	4PM	4PM
5PM	5PM	5PM	5PM
6PM	6PM	6PM	6PM
7PM	7PM	7PM	7PM
8PM	8PM	8PM	8PM
9PM	9PM	9PM	9PM
10PM	10PM	10PM	10PM

WEEK:

FRIDAY	SATURDAY	SUNDAY
5AM	5AM	5AM
6AM	6AM	6AM
7AM	7AM	7AM
8AM	8AM	8AM
9AM	9AM	9AM
10AM	10AM	10AM
11AM	11AM	11AM
12PM	12PM	12PM
1PM	1PM	1PM
2PM	2PM	2PM
3PM	3PM	3PM
4PM	4PM	4PM
5PM	5PM	5PM
6PM	6PM	6PM
7PM	7PM	7PM
8PM	8PM	8PM
9PM	9PM	9PM
10PM	10PM	10PM

WEEKLY TO DO

Weekly Goals for

TOP 3

NOTES:

MANIFESTATIONS:

IMPORTANT DATE EVENTS

/
/
/
/
/
/

GOOD LIFE Made Easy

"You educate a man; you educate a man. You educate a woman; you educate a generation." - Brigham Young

Weekly TO DO LIST

Monday

Tuesday

Wednesday

Thursday

Friday

Saturday

Sunday

Bonus

GOOD LIFE

Weekly Plans

MONDAY	TUESDAY	WEDNESDAY	THURSDAY
5AM	5AM	5AM	5AM
6AM	6AM	6AM	6AM
7AM	7AM	7AM	7AM
8AM	8AM	8AM	8AM
9AM	9AM	9AM	9AM
10AM	10AM	10AM	10AM
11AM	11AM	11AM	11AM
12PM	12PM	12PM	12PM
1PM	1PM	1PM	1PM
2PM	2PM	2PM	2PM
3PM	3PM	3PM	3PM
4PM	4PM	4PM	4PM
5PM	5PM	5PM	5PM
6PM	6PM	6PM	6PM
7PM	7PM	7PM	7PM
8PM	8PM	8PM	8PM
9PM	9PM	9PM	9PM
10PM	10PM	10PM	10PM

WEEK:

FRIDAY	SATURDAY	SUNDAY
5AM	5AM	5AM
6AM	6AM	6AM
7AM	7AM	7AM
8AM	8AM	8AM
9AM	9AM	9AM
10AM	10AM	10AM
11AM	11AM	11AM
12PM	12PM	12PM
1PM	1PM	1PM
2PM	2PM	2PM
3PM	3PM	3PM
4PM	4PM	4PM
5PM	5PM	5PM
6PM	6PM	6PM
7PM	7PM	7PM
8PM	8PM	8PM
9PM	9PM	9PM
10PM	10PM	10PM

WEEKLY TO DO

Weekly Goals for

TOP 3

-
-
-

NOTES:

MANIFESTATIONS:

GOOD LIFE
Made Easy

"Women must learn to play the game as men do." - Eleanor Roosevelt

IMPORTANT DATE EVENTS

/
/
/
/
/
/

Weekly
TO DO LIST

Monday

Tuesday

Wednesday

Thursday

Friday

Saturday

Sunday

Bonus

GOOD LIFE Weekly Plans

MONDAY	TUESDAY	WEDNESDAY	THURSDAY
5AM	5AM	5AM	5AM
6AM	6AM	6AM	6AM
7AM	7AM	7AM	7AM
8AM	8AM	8AM	8AM
9AM	9AM	9AM	9AM
10AM	10AM	10AM	10AM
11AM	11AM	11AM	11AM
12PM	12PM	12PM	12PM
1PM	1PM	1PM	1PM
2PM	2PM	2PM	2PM
3PM	3PM	3PM	3PM
4PM	4PM	4PM	4PM
5PM	5PM	5PM	5PM
6PM	6PM	6PM	6PM
7PM	7PM	7PM	7PM
8PM	8PM	8PM	8PM
9PM	9PM	9PM	9PM
10PM	10PM	10PM	10PM

WEEK:

FRIDAY	SATURDAY	SUNDAY
5AM	5AM	5AM
6AM	6AM	6AM
7AM	7AM	7AM
8AM	8AM	8AM
9AM	9AM	9AM
10AM	10AM	10AM
11AM	11AM	11AM
12PM	12PM	12PM
1PM	1PM	1PM
2PM	2PM	2PM
3PM	3PM	3PM
4PM	4PM	4PM
5PM	5PM	5PM
6PM	6PM	6PM
7PM	7PM	7PM
8PM	8PM	8PM
9PM	9PM	9PM
10PM	10PM	10PM

WEEKLY TO DO

Weekly Goals for

TOP 3

- ______________________
- ______________________
- ______________________

NOTES:

- ______________________
- ______________________
- ______________________
- ______________________
- ______________________
- ______________________
- ______________________
- ______________________
- ______________________
- ______________________

MANIFESTATIONS:

GOOD LIFE
Made Easy

"If it doesn't scare you, you're probably not dreaming big enough.
Tory Burch"

IMPORTANT DATE EVENTS

/ ______________________
/ ______________________
/ ______________________
/ ______________________
/ ______________________
/ ______________________

Weekly
TO DO LIST

Monday

Tuesday

Wednesday

Thursday

Friday

Saturday

Sunday

Bonus

GOOD LIFE

Weekly Plans

MONDAY	TUESDAY	WEDNESDAY	THURSDAY
5AM	5AM	5AM	5AM
6AM	6AM	6AM	6AM
7AM	7AM	7AM	7AM
8AM	8AM	8AM	8AM
9AM	9AM	9AM	9AM
10AM	10AM	10AM	10AM
11AM	11AM	11AM	11AM
12PM	12PM	12PM	12PM
1PM	1PM	1PM	1PM
2PM	2PM	2PM	2PM
3PM	3PM	3PM	3PM
4PM	4PM	4PM	4PM
5PM	5PM	5PM	5PM
6PM	6PM	6PM	6PM
7PM	7PM	7PM	7PM
8PM	8PM	8PM	8PM
9PM	9PM	9PM	9PM
10PM	10PM	10PM	10PM

WEEK:

FRIDAY	SATURDAY	SUNDAY
5AM	5AM	5AM
6AM	6AM	6AM
7AM	7AM	7AM
8AM	8AM	8AM
9AM	9AM	9AM
10AM	10AM	10AM
11AM	11AM	11AM
12PM	12PM	12PM
1PM	1PM	1PM
2PM	2PM	2PM
3PM	3PM	3PM
4PM	4PM	4PM
5PM	5PM	5PM
6PM	6PM	6PM
7PM	7PM	7PM
8PM	8PM	8PM
9PM	9PM	9PM
10PM	10PM	10PM

WEEKLY TO DO

GOOD LIFE

Monthly Plans

NOTES	MONDAY	TUESDAY	WEDNESDAY

MONTH:

THURSDAY	FRIDAY	SATURDAY	SUNDAY

Monthly BUDGET

INCOME	EXPECTED	ACTUAL	DIFFERENCE
HOME EXPENSES			
BUSINESS EXPENSES			

Monthly BUDGET

ADDITIONAL EXPENSES	EXPECTED	ACTUAL	DIFFERENCE

Payment TRACKER

BILL	DUE	$	J	F	M	A	M	J	J	A	S	O	N	D

Self-Development for the month

Books to read this month:

- ○ ______________________
- ○ ______________________
- ○ ______________________

CHAPTERS READ:

MONTHLY HABIT TRACKER

	M	T	W	T	F	S	S

Morning Routine	*Evening Routine*

Monthly Goals
CHECK

JAN	FEB	MAR	APR	MAY	JUN	JUL	AUG	SEP	OCT	NOV	DEC

GOAL:

DEADLINE

DATE ACHIEVED

IMPORTANT STEPS:

- ○ ______
- ○ ______
- ○ ______
- ○ ______
- ○ ______
- ○ ______

Manifestations for THIS month:

"Whatever you hold in your mind on a consistent basis is exactly what you will experience in your life." - Tony Robbins

GIRL
BOSS
Hustle

Notes

Girl Code
Boss Up
NOT THAT KIND OF GIRL
EMPOWERED WOMEN
GIRL BOSS

Weekly Goals for

TOP 3

-
-
-

NOTES:

MANIFESTATIONS:

GOOD LIFE Made Easy

"There is no gate, no lock, no bolt that you can set upon the freedom of my mind." - Virginia Woolf

IMPORTANT DATE EVENTS

/

/

/

/

/

/

Weekly
TO DO LIST

Monday

Tuesday

Wednesday

Thursday

Friday

Saturday

Sunday

Bonus

GOOD LIFE

Weekly Plans

MONDAY	TUESDAY	WEDNESDAY	THURSDAY
5AM	5AM	5AM	5AM
6AM	6AM	6AM	6AM
7AM	7AM	7AM	7AM
8AM	8AM	8AM	8AM
9AM	9AM	9AM	9AM
10AM	10AM	10AM	10AM
11AM	11AM	11AM	11AM
12PM	12PM	12PM	12PM
1PM	1PM	1PM	1PM
2PM	2PM	2PM	2PM
3PM	3PM	3PM	3PM
4PM	4PM	4PM	4PM
5PM	5PM	5PM	5PM
6PM	6PM	6PM	6PM
7PM	7PM	7PM	7PM
8PM	8PM	8PM	8PM
9PM	9PM	9PM	9PM
10PM	10PM	10PM	10PM

WEEK:

FRIDAY	SATURDAY	SUNDAY
5AM	5AM	5AM
6AM	6AM	6AM
7AM	7AM	7AM
8AM	8AM	8AM
9AM	9AM	9AM
10AM	10AM	10AM
11AM	11AM	11AM
12PM	12PM	12PM
1PM	1PM	1PM
2PM	2PM	2PM
3PM	3PM	3PM
4PM	4PM	4PM
5PM	5PM	5PM
6PM	6PM	6PM
7PM	7PM	7PM
8PM	8PM	8PM
9PM	9PM	9PM
10PM	10PM	10PM

WEEKLY TO DO

Weekly Goals for

TOP 3

-
-
-

NOTES:

MANIFESTATIONS:

GOOD LIFE Made Easy

"Define success on your own terms, achieve it by your own rules, and build a life you're proud to live." - Anne Sweeny

IMPORTANT DATE EVENTS

/

/

/

/

/

/

Weekly TO DO LIST

Monday

Tuesday

Wednesday

Thursday

Friday

Saturday

Sunday

Bonus

GOOD LIFE Weekly Plans

MONDAY	TUESDAY	WEDNESDAY	THURSDAY
5AM	5AM	5AM	5AM
6AM	6AM	6AM	6AM
7AM	7AM	7AM	7AM
8AM	8AM	8AM	8AM
9AM	9AM	9AM	9AM
10AM	10AM	10AM	10AM
11AM	11AM	11AM	11AM
12PM	12PM	12PM	12PM
1PM	1PM	1PM	1PM
2PM	2PM	2PM	2PM
3PM	3PM	3PM	3PM
4PM	4PM	4PM	4PM
5PM	5PM	5PM	5PM
6PM	6PM	6PM	6PM
7PM	7PM	7PM	7PM
8PM	8PM	8PM	8PM
9PM	9PM	9PM	9PM
10PM	10PM	10PM	10PM

WEEK:

FRIDAY	SATURDAY	SUNDAY
5AM	5AM	5AM
6AM	6AM	6AM
7AM	7AM	7AM
8AM	8AM	8AM
9AM	9AM	9AM
10AM	10AM	10AM
11AM	11AM	11AM
12PM	12PM	12PM
1PM	1PM	1PM
2PM	2PM	2PM
3PM	3PM	3PM
4PM	4PM	4PM
5PM	5PM	5PM
6PM	6PM	6PM
7PM	7PM	7PM
8PM	8PM	8PM
9PM	9PM	9PM
10PM	10PM	10PM

WEEKLY TO DO

Weekly Goals for

TOP 3

NOTES:

MANIFESTATIONS:

GOOD LIFE Made Easy

"Delete the negative; accentuate the positive." - Donna Karan

IMPORTANT DATE EVENTS

/

/

/

/

/

/

Weekly TO DO LIST

Monday

Tuesday

Wednesday

Thursday

Friday

Saturday

Sunday

Bonus

GOOD LIFE Weekly Plans

MONDAY	TUESDAY	WEDNESDAY	THURSDAY
5AM	5AM	5AM	5AM
6AM	6AM	6AM	6AM
7AM	7AM	7AM	7AM
8AM	8AM	8AM	8AM
9AM	9AM	9AM	9AM
10AM	10AM	10AM	10AM
11AM	11AM	11AM	11AM
12PM	12PM	12PM	12PM
1PM	1PM	1PM	1PM
2PM	2PM	2PM	2PM
3PM	3PM	3PM	3PM
4PM	4PM	4PM	4PM
5PM	5PM	5PM	5PM
6PM	6PM	6PM	6PM
7PM	7PM	7PM	7PM
8PM	8PM	8PM	8PM
9PM	9PM	9PM	9PM
10PM	10PM	10PM	10PM

WEEK:

FRIDAY	SATURDAY	SUNDAY
5AM	5AM	5AM
6AM	6AM	6AM
7AM	7AM	7AM
8AM	8AM	8AM
9AM	9AM	9AM
10AM	10AM	10AM
11AM	11AM	11AM
12PM	12PM	12PM
1PM	1PM	1PM
2PM	2PM	2PM
3PM	3PM	3PM
4PM	4PM	4PM
5PM	5PM	5PM
6PM	6PM	6PM
7PM	7PM	7PM
8PM	8PM	8PM
9PM	9PM	9PM
10PM	10PM	10PM

WEEKLY TO DO

Weekly Goals for

TOP 3

-
-
-

NOTES:

MANIFESTATIONS:

GOOD LIFE Made Easy

"I alone cannot change the world, but I can cast a stone across the waters to create many ripples." - Mother Teresa

IMPORTANT DATE EVENTS

/
/
/
/
/
/

Weekly TO DO LIST

Monday

Tuesday

Wednesday

Thursday

Friday

Saturday

Sunday

Bonus

GOOD LIFE Weekly Plans

MONDAY	TUESDAY	WEDNESDAY	THURSDAY
5AM	5AM	5AM	5AM
6AM	6AM	6AM	6AM
7AM	7AM	7AM	7AM
8AM	8AM	8AM	8AM
9AM	9AM	9AM	9AM
10AM	10AM	10AM	10AM
11AM	11AM	11AM	11AM
12PM	12PM	12PM	12PM
1PM	1PM	1PM	1PM
2PM	2PM	2PM	2PM
3PM	3PM	3PM	3PM
4PM	4PM	4PM	4PM
5PM	5PM	5PM	5PM
6PM	6PM	6PM	6PM
7PM	7PM	7PM	7PM
8PM	8PM	8PM	8PM
9PM	9PM	9PM	9PM
10PM	10PM	10PM	10PM

WEEK:

FRIDAY	SATURDAY	SUNDAY
5AM	5AM	5AM
6AM	6AM	6AM
7AM	7AM	7AM
8AM	8AM	8AM
9AM	9AM	9AM
10AM	10AM	10AM
11AM	11AM	11AM
12PM	12PM	12PM
1PM	1PM	1PM
2PM	2PM	2PM
3PM	3PM	3PM
4PM	4PM	4PM
5PM	5PM	5PM
6PM	6PM	6PM
7PM	7PM	7PM
8PM	8PM	8PM
9PM	9PM	9PM
10PM	10PM	10PM

WEEKLY TO DO

Weekly Goals for

TOP 3

- ______
- ______
- ______

NOTES:

- ______
- ______
- ______
- ______
- ______
- ______
- ______
- ______
- ______
- ______

MANIFESTATIONS:

GOOD LIFE Made Easy

"It's never too late to make a comeback."
Christina Katz

IMPORTANT DATE EVENTS

/ ______
/ ______
/ ______
/ ______
/ ______
/ ______

Weekly TO DO LIST

Monday

Tuesday

Wednesday

Thursday

Friday

Saturday

Sunday

Bonus

GOOD LIFE Weekly Plans

MONDAY	TUESDAY	WEDNESDAY	THURSDAY
5AM	5AM	5AM	5AM
6AM	6AM	6AM	6AM
7AM	7AM	7AM	7AM
8AM	8AM	8AM	8AM
9AM	9AM	9AM	9AM
10AM	10AM	10AM	10AM
11AM	11AM	11AM	11AM
12PM	12PM	12PM	12PM
1PM	1PM	1PM	1PM
2PM	2PM	2PM	2PM
3PM	3PM	3PM	3PM
4PM	4PM	4PM	4PM
5PM	5PM	5PM	5PM
6PM	6PM	6PM	6PM
7PM	7PM	7PM	7PM
8PM	8PM	8PM	8PM
9PM	9PM	9PM	9PM
10PM	10PM	10PM	10PM

WEEK:

FRIDAY	SATURDAY	SUNDAY
5AM	5AM	5AM
6AM	6AM	6AM
7AM	7AM	7AM
8AM	8AM	8AM
9AM	9AM	9AM
10AM	10AM	10AM
11AM	11AM	11AM
12PM	12PM	12PM
1PM	1PM	1PM
2PM	2PM	2PM
3PM	3PM	3PM
4PM	4PM	4PM
5PM	5PM	5PM
6PM	6PM	6PM
7PM	7PM	7PM
8PM	8PM	8PM
9PM	9PM	9PM
10PM	10PM	10PM

WEEKLY TO DO

GOOD LIFE

Monthly Plans

NOTES

MONDAY

TUESDAY

WEDNESDAY

MONTH:

THURSDAY	FRIDAY	SATURDAY	SUNDAY

Monthly BUDGET

INCOME	EXPECTED	ACTUAL	DIFFERENCE
HOME EXPENSES			
BUSINESS EXPENSES			

Monthly BUDGET

ADDITIONAL EXPENSES	EXPECTED	ACTUAL	DIFFERENCE

Payment TRACKER

BILL	DUE	$	J	F	M	A	M	J	J	A	S	O	N	D

Self-Development for the month

Books to read this month:

- ○ ______________________________
- ○ ______________________________
- ○ ______________________________

CHAPTERS READ:

MONTHLY HABIT TRACKER

	M	T	W	T	F	S	S

Morning Routine	*Evening Routine*

Monthly Goals CHECK

JAN	FEB	MAR	APR	MAY	JUN	JUL	AUG	SEP	OCT	NOV	DEC

GOAL:

DEADLINE

DATE ACHIEVED

IMPORTANT STEPS:

- ______
- ______
- ______
- ______
- ______
- ______

Manifestations for THIS month:

"Don't look at your feet to see if you are doing it right. Just dance." - Anne Lamott

GIRL
BOSS
Hustle

Notes

Girl Code
Boss Up
NOT THAT KIND OF GIRL
EMPOWERED WOMEN
GIRL BOSS

Weekly Goals for

TOP 3

-
-
-

NOTES:

MANIFESTATIONS:

GOOD LIFE Made Easy

"Only do what your heart tells you."
Princess Diana

IMPORTANT DATE EVENTS

/
/
/
/
/
/

Weekly TO DO LIST

Monday

Tuesday

Wednesday

Thursday

Friday

Saturday

Sunday

Bonus

GOOD LIFE Weekly Plans

MONDAY	TUESDAY	WEDNESDAY	THURSDAY
5AM	5AM	5AM	5AM
6AM	6AM	6AM	6AM
7AM	7AM	7AM	7AM
8AM	8AM	8AM	8AM
9AM	9AM	9AM	9AM
10AM	10AM	10AM	10AM
11AM	11AM	11AM	11AM
12PM	12PM	12PM	12PM
1PM	1PM	1PM	1PM
2PM	2PM	2PM	2PM
3PM	3PM	3PM	3PM
4PM	4PM	4PM	4PM
5PM	5PM	5PM	5PM
6PM	6PM	6PM	6PM
7PM	7PM	7PM	7PM
8PM	8PM	8PM	8PM
9PM	9PM	9PM	9PM
10PM	10PM	10PM	10PM

WEEK:

FRIDAY	SATURDAY	SUNDAY
5AM	5AM	5AM
6AM	6AM	6AM
7AM	7AM	7AM
8AM	8AM	8AM
9AM	9AM	9AM
10AM	10AM	10AM
11AM	11AM	11AM
12PM	12PM	12PM
1PM	1PM	1PM
2PM	2PM	2PM
3PM	3PM	3PM
4PM	4PM	4PM
5PM	5PM	5PM
6PM	6PM	6PM
7PM	7PM	7PM
8PM	8PM	8PM
9PM	9PM	9PM
10PM	10PM	10PM

WEEKLY TO DO

Weekly Goals for

TOP 3

-
-
-

NOTES:

MANIFESTATIONS:

IMPORTANT DATE EVENTS

/
/
/
/
/
/

GOOD LIFE Made Easy

"Always remember that you are absolutely unique. Just like everyone else."
Margaret Mead

Weekly
TO DO LIST

Monday

Tuesday

Wednesday

Thursday

Friday

Saturday

Sunday

Bonus

GOOD LIFE Weekly Plans

MONDAY	TUESDAY	WEDNESDAY	THURSDAY
5AM	5AM	5AM	5AM
6AM	6AM	6AM	6AM
7AM	7AM	7AM	7AM
8AM	8AM	8AM	8AM
9AM	9AM	9AM	9AM
10AM	10AM	10AM	10AM
11AM	11AM	11AM	11AM
12PM	12PM	12PM	12PM
1PM	1PM	1PM	1PM
2PM	2PM	2PM	2PM
3PM	3PM	3PM	3PM
4PM	4PM	4PM	4PM
5PM	5PM	5PM	5PM
6PM	6PM	6PM	6PM
7PM	7PM	7PM	7PM
8PM	8PM	8PM	8PM
9PM	9PM	9PM	9PM
10PM	10PM	10PM	10PM

WEEK:

FRIDAY	SATURDAY	SUNDAY
5AM	5AM	5AM
6AM	6AM	6AM
7AM	7AM	7AM
8AM	8AM	8AM
9AM	9AM	9AM
10AM	10AM	10AM
11AM	11AM	11AM
12PM	12PM	12PM
1PM	1PM	1PM
2PM	2PM	2PM
3PM	3PM	3PM
4PM	4PM	4PM
5PM	5PM	5PM
6PM	6PM	6PM
7PM	7PM	7PM
8PM	8PM	8PM
9PM	9PM	9PM
10PM	10PM	10PM

WEEKLY TO DO

Weekly Goals for

TOP 3

-
-
-

NOTES:

MANIFESTATIONS:

GOOD LIFE
Made Easy

"Faith is the strength by which a shattered world shall emerge into the light."
Helen Keller

IMPORTANT DATE EVENTS

/
/
/
/
/
/

Weekly TO DO LIST

Monday

Tuesday

Wednesday

Thursday

Friday

Saturday

Sunday

Bonus

GOOD LIFE

Weekly Plans

MONDAY	TUESDAY	WEDNESDAY	THURSDAY
5AM	5AM	5AM	5AM
6AM	6AM	6AM	6AM
7AM	7AM	7AM	7AM
8AM	8AM	8AM	8AM
9AM	9AM	9AM	9AM
10AM	10AM	10AM	10AM
11AM	11AM	11AM	11AM
12PM	12PM	12PM	12PM
1PM	1PM	1PM	1PM
2PM	2PM	2PM	2PM
3PM	3PM	3PM	3PM
4PM	4PM	4PM	4PM
5PM	5PM	5PM	5PM
6PM	6PM	6PM	6PM
7PM	7PM	7PM	7PM
8PM	8PM	8PM	8PM
9PM	9PM	9PM	9PM
10PM	10PM	10PM	10PM

WEEK:

FRIDAY	SATURDAY	SUNDAY
5AM	5AM	5AM
6AM	6AM	6AM
7AM	7AM	7AM
8AM	8AM	8AM
9AM	9AM	9AM
10AM	10AM	10AM
11AM	11AM	11AM
12PM	12PM	12PM
1PM	1PM	1PM
2PM	2PM	2PM
3PM	3PM	3PM
4PM	4PM	4PM
5PM	5PM	5PM
6PM	6PM	6PM
7PM	7PM	7PM
8PM	8PM	8PM
9PM	9PM	9PM
10PM	10PM	10PM

WEEKLY TO DO

Weekly Goals for

TOP 3

NOTES:

MANIFESTATIONS:

GOOD LIFE Made Easy

"When you're building a business, you're either all in, or you're not."
Barbara Corcoran

IMPORTANT DATE EVENTS

/
/
/
/
/
/

Weekly TO DO LIST

Monday

Tuesday

Wednesday

Thursday

Friday

Saturday

Sunday

Bonus

GOOD LIFE *Weekly Plans*

MONDAY	TUESDAY	WEDNESDAY	THURSDAY
5AM	5AM	5AM	5AM
6AM	6AM	6AM	6AM
7AM	7AM	7AM	7AM
8AM	8AM	8AM	8AM
9AM	9AM	9AM	9AM
10AM	10AM	10AM	10AM
11AM	11AM	11AM	11AM
12PM	12PM	12PM	12PM
1PM	1PM	1PM	1PM
2PM	2PM	2PM	2PM
3PM	3PM	3PM	3PM
4PM	4PM	4PM	4PM
5PM	5PM	5PM	5PM
6PM	6PM	6PM	6PM
7PM	7PM	7PM	7PM
8PM	8PM	8PM	8PM
9PM	9PM	9PM	9PM
10PM	10PM	10PM	10PM

WEEK:

FRIDAY	SATURDAY	SUNDAY
5AM	5AM	5AM
6AM	6AM	6AM
7AM	7AM	7AM
8AM	8AM	8AM
9AM	9AM	9AM
10AM	10AM	10AM
11AM	11AM	11AM
12PM	12PM	12PM
1PM	1PM	1PM
2PM	2PM	2PM
3PM	3PM	3PM
4PM	4PM	4PM
5PM	5PM	5PM
6PM	6PM	6PM
7PM	7PM	7PM
8PM	8PM	8PM
9PM	9PM	9PM
10PM	10PM	10PM

WEEKLY TO DO

GOOD LIFE

Monthly Plans

NOTES	MONDAY	TUESDAY	WEDNESDAY

MONTH:

THURSDAY	FRIDAY	SATURDAY	SUNDAY

Monthly BUDGET

INCOME	EXPECTED	ACTUAL	DIFFERENCE
HOME EXPENSES			
BUSINESS EXPENSES			

Monthly BUDGET

ADDITIONAL EXPENSES	EXPECTED	ACTUAL	DIFFERENCE

Payment TRACKER

BILL	DUE	$	J	F	M	A	M	J	J	A	S	O	N	D

Self-Development for the month

Books to read this month:

CHAPTERS READ:

MONTHLY HABIT TRACKER

M T W T F S S

Morning Routine	Evening Routine

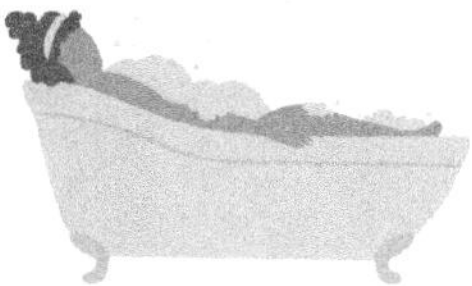

Monthly Goals
CHECK

JAN	FEB	MAR	APR	MAY	JUN	JUL	AUG	SEP	OCT	NOV	DEC

GOAL:

DEADLINE

DATE ACHIEVED

IMPORTANT STEPS:

Manifestations for THIS month:

"The future belongs to those who believe in the beauty of their own dreams." - Franklin D. Roosevelt

GIRL
BOSS
Hustle

Notes

Girl Code
Boss Up
NOT THAT KIND OF GIRL
EMPOWERED WOMEN
GIRL BOSS

Weekly Goals for

TOP 3

NOTES:

MANIFESTATIONS:

GOOD LIFE Made Easy

"Don't waste a single second. Just move forward as fast as you can, and go for it."
Rebecca Woodcock

IMPORTANT DATE EVENTS

/
/
/
/
/
/

Weekly
TO DO LIST

Monday

Tuesday

Wednesday

Thursday

Friday

Saturday

Sunday

Bonus

GOOD LIFE *Weekly Plans*

MONDAY	TUESDAY	WEDNESDAY	THURSDAY
5AM	5AM	5AM	5AM
6AM	6AM	6AM	6AM
7AM	7AM	7AM	7AM
8AM	8AM	8AM	8AM
9AM	9AM	9AM	9AM
10AM	10AM	10AM	10AM
11AM	11AM	11AM	11AM
12PM	12PM	12PM	12PM
1PM	1PM	1PM	1PM
2PM	2PM	2PM	2PM
3PM	3PM	3PM	3PM
4PM	4PM	4PM	4PM
5PM	5PM	5PM	5PM
6PM	6PM	6PM	6PM
7PM	7PM	7PM	7PM
8PM	8PM	8PM	8PM
9PM	9PM	9PM	9PM
10PM	10PM	10PM	10PM

WEEK:

FRIDAY	SATURDAY	SUNDAY
5AM	5AM	5AM
6AM	6AM	6AM
7AM	7AM	7AM
8AM	8AM	8AM
9AM	9AM	9AM
10AM	10AM	10AM
11AM	11AM	11AM
12PM	12PM	12PM
1PM	1PM	1PM
2PM	2PM	2PM
3PM	3PM	3PM
4PM	4PM	4PM
5PM	5PM	5PM
6PM	6PM	6PM
7PM	7PM	7PM
8PM	8PM	8PM
9PM	9PM	9PM
10PM	10PM	10PM

WEEKLY TO DO

Weekly Goals for

TOP 3

•
•
•

NOTES:

MANIFESTATIONS:

IMPORTANT DATE EVENTS

/
/
/
/
/
/

GOOD LIFE Made Easy

"You have to do what you dream of doing, even while you're afraid."
Arianna Huffington

Weekly TO DO LIST

Monday

Tuesday

Wednesday

Thursday

Friday

Saturday

Sunday

Bonus

GOOD LIFE *Weekly Plans*

MONDAY	TUESDAY	WEDNESDAY	THURSDAY
5AM	5AM	5AM	5AM
6AM	6AM	6AM	6AM
7AM	7AM	7AM	7AM
8AM	8AM	8AM	8AM
9AM	9AM	9AM	9AM
10AM	10AM	10AM	10AM
11AM	11AM	11AM	11AM
12PM	12PM	12PM	12PM
1PM	1PM	1PM	1PM
2PM	2PM	2PM	2PM
3PM	3PM	3PM	3PM
4PM	4PM	4PM	4PM
5PM	5PM	5PM	5PM
6PM	6PM	6PM	6PM
7PM	7PM	7PM	7PM
8PM	8PM	8PM	8PM
9PM	9PM	9PM	9PM
10PM	10PM	10PM	10PM

WEEK:

FRIDAY	SATURDAY	SUNDAY
5AM	5AM	5AM
6AM	6AM	6AM
7AM	7AM	7AM
8AM	8AM	8AM
9AM	9AM	9AM
10AM	10AM	10AM
11AM	11AM	11AM
12PM	12PM	12PM
1PM	1PM	1PM
2PM	2PM	2PM
3PM	3PM	3PM
4PM	4PM	4PM
5PM	5PM	5PM
6PM	6PM	6PM
7PM	7PM	7PM
8PM	8PM	8PM
9PM	9PM	9PM
10PM	10PM	10PM

WEEKLY TO DO

Weekly Goals for

TOP 3

-
-
-

NOTES:

MANIFESTATIONS:

GOOD LIFE Made Easy

"Happiness is the gradual realization of a worthy ideal or goal."
Florence Nightingale

IMPORTANT DATE EVENTS

/
/
/
/
/
/

Weekly TO DO LIST

Monday

Tuesday

Wednesday

Thursday

Friday

Saturday

Sunday

Bonus

GOOD LIFE Weekly Plans

MONDAY	TUESDAY	WEDNESDAY	THURSDAY
5AM	5AM	5AM	5AM
6AM	6AM	6AM	6AM
7AM	7AM	7AM	7AM
8AM	8AM	8AM	8AM
9AM	9AM	9AM	9AM
10AM	10AM	10AM	10AM
11AM	11AM	11AM	11AM
12PM	12PM	12PM	12PM
1PM	1PM	1PM	1PM
2PM	2PM	2PM	2PM
3PM	3PM	3PM	3PM
4PM	4PM	4PM	4PM
5PM	5PM	5PM	5PM
6PM	6PM	6PM	6PM
7PM	7PM	7PM	7PM
8PM	8PM	8PM	8PM
9PM	9PM	9PM	9PM
10PM	10PM	10PM	10PM

WEEK:

FRIDAY	SATURDAY	SUNDAY
5AM	5AM	5AM
6AM	6AM	6AM
7AM	7AM	7AM
8AM	8AM	8AM
9AM	9AM	9AM
10AM	10AM	10AM
11AM	11AM	11AM
12PM	12PM	12PM
1PM	1PM	1PM
2PM	2PM	2PM
3PM	3PM	3PM
4PM	4PM	4PM
5PM	5PM	5PM
6PM	6PM	6PM
7PM	7PM	7PM
8PM	8PM	8PM
9PM	9PM	9PM
10PM	10PM	10PM

WEEKLY TO DO

Weekly Goals for

TOP 3

NOTES:

MANIFESTATIONS:

GOOD LIFE Made Easy

"If it doesn't scare you, you're probably not dreaming big enough."
Tory Burch

IMPORTANT DATE EVENTS

/

/

/

/

/

/

Weekly
TO DO LIST

Monday

Tuesday

Wednesday

Thursday

Friday

Saturday

Sunday

Bonus

GOOD LIFE
Weekly Plans

MONDAY	TUESDAY	WEDNESDAY	THURSDAY
5AM	5AM	5AM	5AM
6AM	6AM	6AM	6AM
7AM	7AM	7AM	7AM
8AM	8AM	8AM	8AM
9AM	9AM	9AM	9AM
10AM	10AM	10AM	10AM
11AM	11AM	11AM	11AM
12PM	12PM	12PM	12PM
1PM	1PM	1PM	1PM
2PM	2PM	2PM	2PM
3PM	3PM	3PM	3PM
4PM	4PM	4PM	4PM
5PM	5PM	5PM	5PM
6PM	6PM	6PM	6PM
7PM	7PM	7PM	7PM
8PM	8PM	8PM	8PM
9PM	9PM	9PM	9PM
10PM	10PM	10PM	10PM

WEEK:

FRIDAY	SATURDAY	SUNDAY
5AM	5AM	5AM
6AM	6AM	6AM
7AM	7AM	7AM
8AM	8AM	8AM
9AM	9AM	9AM
10AM	10AM	10AM
11AM	11AM	11AM
12PM	12PM	12PM
1PM	1PM	1PM
2PM	2PM	2PM
3PM	3PM	3PM
4PM	4PM	4PM
5PM	5PM	5PM
6PM	6PM	6PM
7PM	7PM	7PM
8PM	8PM	8PM
9PM	9PM	9PM
10PM	10PM	10PM

WEEKLY TO DO

Weekly Goals for

TOP 3

-
-
-

NOTES:

MANIFESTATIONS:

GOOD LIFE Made Easy

"I am not afraid...I was born to do this."
Joan Of Arc

IMPORTANT DATE EVENTS

/
/
/
/
/
/

Weekly TO DO LIST

Monday

Tuesday

Wednesday

Thursday

Friday

Saturday

Sunday

Bonus

GOOD LIFE *Weekly Plans*

MONDAY	TUESDAY	WEDNESDAY	THURSDAY
5AM	5AM	5AM	5AM
6AM	6AM	6AM	6AM
7AM	7AM	7AM	7AM
8AM	8AM	8AM	8AM
9AM	9AM	9AM	9AM
10AM	10AM	10AM	10AM
11AM	11AM	11AM	11AM
12PM	12PM	12PM	12PM
1PM	1PM	1PM	1PM
2PM	2PM	2PM	2PM
3PM	3PM	3PM	3PM
4PM	4PM	4PM	4PM
5PM	5PM	5PM	5PM
6PM	6PM	6PM	6PM
7PM	7PM	7PM	7PM
8PM	8PM	8PM	8PM
9PM	9PM	9PM	9PM
10PM	10PM	10PM	10PM

WEEK:

FRIDAY	SATURDAY	SUNDAY
5AM	5AM	5AM
6AM	6AM	6AM
7AM	7AM	7AM
8AM	8AM	8AM
9AM	9AM	9AM
10AM	10AM	10AM
11AM	11AM	11AM
12PM	12PM	12PM
1PM	1PM	1PM
2PM	2PM	2PM
3PM	3PM	3PM
4PM	4PM	4PM
5PM	5PM	5PM
6PM	6PM	6PM
7PM	7PM	7PM
8PM	8PM	8PM
9PM	9PM	9PM
10PM	10PM	10PM

WEEKLY TO DO

GOOD LIFE

Monthly Plans

NOTES	MONDAY	TUESDAY	WEDNESDAY

MONTH:

THURSDAY	FRIDAY	SATURDAY	SUNDAY

Monthly BUDGET

INCOME	EXPECTED	ACTUAL	DIFFERENCE
HOME EXPENSES			
BUSINESS EXPENSES			

Monthly BUDGET

ADDITIONAL EXPENSES	EXPECTED	ACTUAL	DIFFERENCE

Payment TRACKER

BILL	DUE	$	J	F	M	A	M	J	J	A	S	O	N	D

Self-Development for the month

Books to read this month:

- ○ ______________________________
- ○ ______________________________
- ○ ______________________________

CHAPTERS READ:

MONTHLY HABIT TRACKER

	M	T	W	T	F	S	S

Morning Routine	*Evening Routine*

Monthly Goals
CHECK

JAN	FEB	MAR	APR	MAY	JUN	JUL	AUG	SEP	OCT	NOV	DEC

GOAL:

DEADLINE

DATE ACHIEVED

IMPORTANT STEPS:

- ______
- ______
- ______
- ______
- ______
- ______

Manifestations for THIS month:

"Nothing is really ours until we share it."
- C.S. Lewis

GIRL BOSS
Hustle

Notes

Girl Code
Boss Up
NOT THAT KIND OF GIRL
EMPOWERED WOMEN
GIRL BOSS

Weekly Goals for

TOP 3

NOTES:

MANIFESTATIONS:

GOOD LIFE Made Easy

"As an entrepreneur, you can always find a solution if you try hard enough."
Lori Greiner

IMPORTANT DATE EVENTS

/
/
/
/
/
/

Weekly
TO DO LIST

Monday

Tuesday

Wednesday

Thursday

Friday

Saturday

Sunday

Bonus

GOOD LIFE *Weekly Plans*

MONDAY	TUESDAY	WEDNESDAY	THURSDAY
5AM	5AM	5AM	5AM
6AM	6AM	6AM	6AM
7AM	7AM	7AM	7AM
8AM	8AM	8AM	8AM
9AM	9AM	9AM	9AM
10AM	10AM	10AM	10AM
11AM	11AM	11AM	11AM
12PM	12PM	12PM	12PM
1PM	1PM	1PM	1PM
2PM	2PM	2PM	2PM
3PM	3PM	3PM	3PM
4PM	4PM	4PM	4PM
5PM	5PM	5PM	5PM
6PM	6PM	6PM	6PM
7PM	7PM	7PM	7PM
8PM	8PM	8PM	8PM
9PM	9PM	9PM	9PM
10PM	10PM	10PM	10PM

WEEK:

FRIDAY	SATURDAY	SUNDAY
5AM	5AM	5AM
6AM	6AM	6AM
7AM	7AM	7AM
8AM	8AM	8AM
9AM	9AM	9AM
10AM	10AM	10AM
11AM	11AM	11AM
12PM	12PM	12PM
1PM	1PM	1PM
2PM	2PM	2PM
3PM	3PM	3PM
4PM	4PM	4PM
5PM	5PM	5PM
6PM	6PM	6PM
7PM	7PM	7PM
8PM	8PM	8PM
9PM	9PM	9PM
10PM	10PM	10PM

WEEKLY TO DO

Weekly Goals for

TOP 3

NOTES:

MANIFESTATIONS:

IMPORTANT DATE EVENTS

/

/

/

/

/

/

GOOD LIFE Made Easy

"Work smart. Get things done. No nonsense.
Move fast.
Susan Wojcicki

Weekly TO DO LIST

Monday

Tuesday

Wednesday

Thursday

Friday

Saturday

Sunday

Bonus

GOOD LIFE *Weekly Plans*

MONDAY	TUESDAY	WEDNESDAY	THURSDAY
5AM	5AM	5AM	5AM
6AM	6AM	6AM	6AM
7AM	7AM	7AM	7AM
8AM	8AM	8AM	8AM
9AM	9AM	9AM	9AM
10AM	10AM	10AM	10AM
11AM	11AM	11AM	11AM
12PM	12PM	12PM	12PM
1PM	1PM	1PM	1PM
2PM	2PM	2PM	2PM
3PM	3PM	3PM	3PM
4PM	4PM	4PM	4PM
5PM	5PM	5PM	5PM
6PM	6PM	6PM	6PM
7PM	7PM	7PM	7PM
8PM	8PM	8PM	8PM
9PM	9PM	9PM	9PM
10PM	10PM	10PM	10PM

WEEK:

FRIDAY	SATURDAY	SUNDAY
5AM	5AM	5AM
6AM	6AM	6AM
7AM	7AM	7AM
8AM	8AM	8AM
9AM	9AM	9AM
10AM	10AM	10AM
11AM	11AM	11AM
12PM	12PM	12PM
1PM	1PM	1PM
2PM	2PM	2PM
3PM	3PM	3PM
4PM	4PM	4PM
5PM	5PM	5PM
6PM	6PM	6PM
7PM	7PM	7PM
8PM	8PM	8PM
9PM	9PM	9PM
10PM	10PM	10PM

WEEKLY TO DO

Weekly Goals for

TOP 3

NOTES:

MANIFESTATIONS:

IMPORTANT DATE EVENTS

GOOD LIFE Made Easy

"It took me quite a long time to develop a voice, and now that I have it, I am not going to be silent." — Madeleine Albright

/

/

/

/

/

/

Weekly TO DO LIST

Monday

Tuesday

Wednesday

Thursday

Friday

Saturday

Sunday

Bonus

GOOD LIFE *Weekly Plans*

MONDAY	TUESDAY	WEDNESDAY	THURSDAY
5AM	5AM	5AM	5AM
6AM	6AM	6AM	6AM
7AM	7AM	7AM	7AM
8AM	8AM	8AM	8AM
9AM	9AM	9AM	9AM
10AM	10AM	10AM	10AM
11AM	11AM	11AM	11AM
12PM	12PM	12PM	12PM
1PM	1PM	1PM	1PM
2PM	2PM	2PM	2PM
3PM	3PM	3PM	3PM
4PM	4PM	4PM	4PM
5PM	5PM	5PM	5PM
6PM	6PM	6PM	6PM
7PM	7PM	7PM	7PM
8PM	8PM	8PM	8PM
9PM	9PM	9PM	9PM
10PM	10PM	10PM	10PM

WEEK:

FRIDAY	SATURDAY	SUNDAY
5AM	5AM	5AM
6AM	6AM	6AM
7AM	7AM	7AM
8AM	8AM	8AM
9AM	9AM	9AM
10AM	10AM	10AM
11AM	11AM	11AM
12PM	12PM	12PM
1PM	1PM	1PM
2PM	2PM	2PM
3PM	3PM	3PM
4PM	4PM	4PM
5PM	5PM	5PM
6PM	6PM	6PM
7PM	7PM	7PM
8PM	8PM	8PM
9PM	9PM	9PM
10PM	10PM	10PM

WEEKLY TO DO

Weekly Goals for

TOP 3

-
-
-

NOTES:

MANIFESTATIONS:

IMPORTANT DATE EVENTS

/
/
/
/
/
/

GOOD LIFE Made Easy

"No one can make you feel inferior without your consent." — Eleanor Roosevelt

Weekly
TO DO LIST

Monday

Tuesday

Wednesday

Thursday

Friday

Saturday

Sunday

Bonus

GOOD LIFE

Monthly Plans

NOTES	MONDAY	TUESDAY	WEDNESDAY

MONTH:

THURSDAY	FRIDAY	SATURDAY	SUNDAY

Monthly BUDGET

INCOME	EXPECTED	ACTUAL	DIFFERENCE
HOME EXPENSES			
BUSINESS EXPENSES			

Monthly BUDGET

ADDITIONAL EXPENSES	EXPECTED	ACTUAL	DIFFERENCE

Payment TRACKER

BILL	DUE	$	J F M A M J J A S O N D

Self-Development for the month

Books to read this month:

- ______________________
- ______________________
- ______________________

CHAPTERS READ:

MONTHLY HABIT TRACKER

M T W T F S S

Morning Routine	Evening Routine

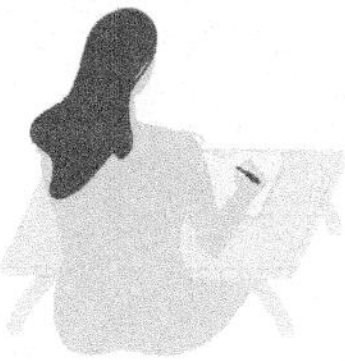

Monthly Goals CHECK

JAN	FEB	MAR	APR	MAY	JUN	JUL	AUG	SEP	OCT	NOV	DEC

GOAL:

DEADLINE

DATE ACHIEVED

IMPORTANT STEPS:

- ○ ____________________
- ○ ____________________
- ○ ____________________
- ○ ____________________
- ○ ____________________
- ○ ____________________

Manifestations for THIS month:

"It is during our darkest moments we must focus to see the light." - Aristotle Onassis

GIRL
BOSS
Hustle

Notes

Girl Code
Boss Up
NOT THAT KIND OF GIRL
EMPOWERED WOMEN
GIRL BOSS

Weekly Goals for

TOP 3

•
•
•

NOTES:

MANIFESTATIONS:

IMPORTANT DATE EVENTS

/
/
/
/
/
/

GOOD LIFE
Made Easy

"Never give up, for that is just the place and time that the tide will turn." — Harriet Beecher Stowe

Weekly
TO DO LIST

Monday

Tuesday

Wednesday

Thursday

Friday

Saturday

Sunday

Bonus

GOOD LIFE *Weekly Plans*

MONDAY	TUESDAY	WEDNESDAY	THURSDAY
5AM	5AM	5AM	5AM
6AM	6AM	6AM	6AM
7AM	7AM	7AM	7AM
8AM	8AM	8AM	8AM
9AM	9AM	9AM	9AM
10AM	10AM	10AM	10AM
11AM	11AM	11AM	11AM
12PM	12PM	12PM	12PM
1PM	1PM	1PM	1PM
2PM	2PM	2PM	2PM
3PM	3PM	3PM	3PM
4PM	4PM	4PM	4PM
5PM	5PM	5PM	5PM
6PM	6PM	6PM	6PM
7PM	7PM	7PM	7PM
8PM	8PM	8PM	8PM
9PM	9PM	9PM	9PM
10PM	10PM	10PM	10PM

WEEK:

FRIDAY	SATURDAY	SUNDAY
5AM	5AM	5AM
6AM	6AM	6AM
7AM	7AM	7AM
8AM	8AM	8AM
9AM	9AM	9AM
10AM	10AM	10AM
11AM	11AM	11AM
12PM	12PM	12PM
1PM	1PM	1PM
2PM	2PM	2PM
3PM	3PM	3PM
4PM	4PM	4PM
5PM	5PM	5PM
6PM	6PM	6PM
7PM	7PM	7PM
8PM	8PM	8PM
9PM	9PM	9PM
10PM	10PM	10PM

WEEKLY TO DO

Weekly Goals for

TOP 3

NOTES:

MANIFESTATIONS:

GOOD LIFE
Made Easy

"The most effective way to do it, is to do it."
— Amelia Earhart.

IMPORTANT DATE EVENTS

/
/
/
/
/
/

Weekly
TO DO LIST

Monday

Tuesday

Wednesday

Thursday

Friday

Saturday

Sunday

Bonus

GOOD LIFE
Weekly Plans

MONDAY	TUESDAY	WEDNESDAY	THURSDAY
5AM	5AM	5AM	5AM
6AM	6AM	6AM	6AM
7AM	7AM	7AM	7AM
8AM	8AM	8AM	8AM
9AM	9AM	9AM	9AM
10AM	10AM	10AM	10AM
11AM	11AM	11AM	11AM
12PM	12PM	12PM	12PM
1PM	1PM	1PM	1PM
2PM	2PM	2PM	2PM
3PM	3PM	3PM	3PM
4PM	4PM	4PM	4PM
5PM	5PM	5PM	5PM
6PM	6PM	6PM	6PM
7PM	7PM	7PM	7PM
8PM	8PM	8PM	8PM
9PM	9PM	9PM	9PM
10PM	10PM	10PM	10PM

WEEK:

FRIDAY	SATURDAY	SUNDAY
5AM	5AM	5AM
6AM	6AM	6AM
7AM	7AM	7AM
8AM	8AM	8AM
9AM	9AM	9AM
10AM	10AM	10AM
11AM	11AM	11AM
12PM	12PM	12PM
1PM	1PM	1PM
2PM	2PM	2PM
3PM	3PM	3PM
4PM	4PM	4PM
5PM	5PM	5PM
6PM	6PM	6PM
7PM	7PM	7PM
8PM	8PM	8PM
9PM	9PM	9PM
10PM	10PM	10PM

WEEKLY TO DO

Weekly Goals for

TOP 3

NOTES:

MANIFESTATIONS:

GOOD LIFE Made Easy

IMPORTANT DATE EVENTS

/

/

/

/

/

/

"You only live once, but if you do it right, once is enough." — Mae West

Weekly
TO DO LIST

Monday

Tuesday

Wednesday

Thursday

Friday

Saturday

Sunday

Bonus

GOOD LIFE *Weekly Plans*

MONDAY	TUESDAY	WEDNESDAY	THURSDAY
5AM	5AM	5AM	5AM
6AM	6AM	6AM	6AM
7AM	7AM	7AM	7AM
8AM	8AM	8AM	8AM
9AM	9AM	9AM	9AM
10AM	10AM	10AM	10AM
11AM	11AM	11AM	11AM
12PM	12PM	12PM	12PM
1PM	1PM	1PM	1PM
2PM	2PM	2PM	2PM
3PM	3PM	3PM	3PM
4PM	4PM	4PM	4PM
5PM	5PM	5PM	5PM
6PM	6PM	6PM	6PM
7PM	7PM	7PM	7PM
8PM	8PM	8PM	8PM
9PM	9PM	9PM	9PM
10PM	10PM	10PM	10PM

WEEK:

FRIDAY	SATURDAY	SUNDAY
5AM	5AM	5AM
6AM	6AM	6AM
7AM	7AM	7AM
8AM	8AM	8AM
9AM	9AM	9AM
10AM	10AM	10AM
11AM	11AM	11AM
12PM	12PM	12PM
1PM	1PM	1PM
2PM	2PM	2PM
3PM	3PM	3PM
4PM	4PM	4PM
5PM	5PM	5PM
6PM	6PM	6PM
7PM	7PM	7PM
8PM	8PM	8PM
9PM	9PM	9PM
10PM	10PM	10PM

WEEKLY TO DO

Weekly Goals for

TOP 3

NOTES:

MANIFESTATIONS:

GOOD LIFE *Made Easy*

"You must learn to be still in the midst of activity and to be vibrantly alive in repose."
— Indira Gandhi

IMPORTANT DATE EVENTS

/

/

/

/

/

/

Weekly TO DO LIST

Monday

Tuesday

Wednesday

Thursday

Friday

Saturday

Sunday

Bonus

GOOD LIFE
Weekly Plans

MONDAY	TUESDAY	WEDNESDAY	THURSDAY
5AM	5AM	5AM	5AM
6AM	6AM	6AM	6AM
7AM	7AM	7AM	7AM
8AM	8AM	8AM	8AM
9AM	9AM	9AM	9AM
10AM	10AM	10AM	10AM
11AM	11AM	11AM	11AM
12PM	12PM	12PM	12PM
1PM	1PM	1PM	1PM
2PM	2PM	2PM	2PM
3PM	3PM	3PM	3PM
4PM	4PM	4PM	4PM
5PM	5PM	5PM	5PM
6PM	6PM	6PM	6PM
7PM	7PM	7PM	7PM
8PM	8PM	8PM	8PM
9PM	9PM	9PM	9PM
10PM	10PM	10PM	10PM

WEEK:

FRIDAY	SATURDAY	SUNDAY
5AM	5AM	5AM
6AM	6AM	6AM
7AM	7AM	7AM
8AM	8AM	8AM
9AM	9AM	9AM
10AM	10AM	10AM
11AM	11AM	11AM
12PM	12PM	12PM
1PM	1PM	1PM
2PM	2PM	2PM
3PM	3PM	3PM
4PM	4PM	4PM
5PM	5PM	5PM
6PM	6PM	6PM
7PM	7PM	7PM
8PM	8PM	8PM
9PM	9PM	9PM
10PM	10PM	10PM

WEEKLY TO DO

Weekly Goals for

TOP 3

NOTES:

MANIFESTATIONS:

GOOD LIFE Made Easy

IMPORTANT DATE EVENTS

/
/
/
/
/
/

"Inspiration comes from within yourself. One has to be positive." - Deep Roy

Weekly
TO DO LIST

Monday	Tuesday	Wednesday	Thursday
○	○	○	○
○	○	○	○
○	○	○	○
○	○	○	○
○	○	○	○
○	○	○	○
○	○	○	○
○	○	○	○
○	○	○	○
○	○	○	○

Friday	Saturday	Sunday	Bonus
○	○	○	○
○	○	○	○
○	○	○	○
○	○	○	○
○	○	○	○
○	○	○	○
○	○	○	○
○	○	○	○
○	○	○	○
○	○	○	○

GOOD LIFE *Weekly Plans*

MONDAY	TUESDAY	WEDNESDAY	THURSDAY
5AM	5AM	5AM	5AM
6AM	6AM	6AM	6AM
7AM	7AM	7AM	7AM
8AM	8AM	8AM	8AM
9AM	9AM	9AM	9AM
10AM	10AM	10AM	10AM
11AM	11AM	11AM	11AM
12PM	12PM	12PM	12PM
1PM	1PM	1PM	1PM
2PM	2PM	2PM	2PM
3PM	3PM	3PM	3PM
4PM	4PM	4PM	4PM
5PM	5PM	5PM	5PM
6PM	6PM	6PM	6PM
7PM	7PM	7PM	7PM
8PM	8PM	8PM	8PM
9PM	9PM	9PM	9PM
10PM	10PM	10PM	10PM

WEEK:

FRIDAY	SATURDAY	SUNDAY
5AM	5AM	5AM
6AM	6AM	6AM
7AM	7AM	7AM
8AM	8AM	8AM
9AM	9AM	9AM
10AM	10AM	10AM
11AM	11AM	11AM
12PM	12PM	12PM
1PM	1PM	1PM
2PM	2PM	2PM
3PM	3PM	3PM
4PM	4PM	4PM
5PM	5PM	5PM
6PM	6PM	6PM
7PM	7PM	7PM
8PM	8PM	8PM
9PM	9PM	9PM
10PM	10PM	10PM

WEEKLY TO DO

Made in the USA
Monee, IL
04 November 2026

67379929R00184